Seven Year Summer

Anna Byrne

For all who travelled this road with me

those who set the stones and held the threshold
those who brought medicine and mystery
the many who were carried and their couriers
those who were friends, for redeeming our foes
for the circle of ancestors and their offshoots
my siblings and soul friends
the guards and the guides

and for those

who did not reach the length
yet added to the breadth
and all who stayed aside me
in the depths

especially

Andrew and Mom

The Uses of Sorrow

(In my sleep I dreamed this poem)
Someone I loved once gave me
a box full of darkness.
It took me years to understand
that this too, was a gift.

- Mary Oliver

Year 1

"Hopefully, in a year, this will all be behind you." The doctor stood and held out his hand. A peace offering.

The same hand had just scribed my treatment plan: Six months of outpatient chemotherapy, blood work three times a week, appointments with the social worker and nutritionist, possible radiation and periodic scans to monitor how this plan was working.

I shook his hand. But as I left his office, his predictions of hair loss and lost fertility, of nausea and needles, fell away from this one final statement: Hopefully, in a year. In a year. Hopefully.

A year? An entire year of my life?

It's June. I am 32 years old. I have Hodgkin's lymphoma.

That was seven years ago.

Year 7

It's late June as Andrew and I drive from Windsor to Toronto on the last leg of our three-week visit. Though it's only been six months since we've moved to British Columbia, a cluster of birthdays and graduations have brought us back to Ontario. It's still early summer but some days, the temperature has reached 30 degrees Celsius with the humidity level.

We arrive, put our bags in the upstairs bedroom, then spend a few hours talking in the living room with Andrew's parents. When we later climb the stairs to bed, there's a voicemail on my phone from Alex, the coordinator of the hospice where I've just begun volunteering. A woman recently admitted to the hospital is requesting support. Am I able to visit? I look at the clock. It's almost midnight — 9 p.m. in British Columbia — and too late to call.

The next morning, I take my coffee, pen and paper outside to the deck and phone Alex. She has only a few details. The client is a woman in her 70s who has renal failure. There is no family involved. Though she has had kidney disease for some time, she is now in the active stages of dying. Her name is Eleanor Davis.

I have only one question. Will I make it in time? I won't be back from Ontario for another five days. Perhaps someone else should visit instead?

"No," says Alex. "It's already Friday. By the time I find someone else and have them begin, you'll be back." I hang up after assuring her that I will visit the first morning I return.

That's how I came to know Eleanor.

Seven Year Summer

1

Port:

A harbour where ships take on or discharge cargo;
An opening for the controlled intake or exhaust of fluids;
A place where vessels reside from storms;
A haven.

Year 1

Four months before my handshake with the doctor, I pulled myself from the Atlantic Ocean onto the eastern shore of Brazil cradling my right arm, which had just broken in three places.

My brother Pete had come to visit me during the last few weeks of an eight-month trip to South Africa, Mozambique and Brazil, where I had volunteered with several organizations working with vulnerable children. The trip had fulfilled my childhood dream of volunteering and travelling overseas. I took a few weeks off from the ministry to travel with Pete to the coast. It was a hot, windy day in the port town where we stayed, so we packed our towels and went to the beach. The water was wild. Standing waist deep, we let the giant waves crash over us. We held hands as we went under, laughing hard and loud like children. Over and over we submerged, surfaced, submerged, surfaced.

After awhile, Pete swam out a little farther while I turned towards shore to towel off. Behind me, a wave stood, rose to the full length of its legs and exploded over me. Wrapped in its arms, I was pulled underwater. I fell at an awkward angle, the side of my face and right shoulder slamming into the ocean floor. While submerged, my ear took in the sound of the crack.

A few hours later, a doctor at the local hospital pulled up the X-ray pictures and pointed, though I could clearly see the thin white lines, drawn like chalk across the silhouette of my skeleton. One wiggled across my upper arm. Another was a piece of bone, splintered up against my skin. When my bones collided from the impact, they acted like tectonic plates under the earth's surface, one forced upward into a tiny mountain. As the doctor motioned to it, the fingers of my left hand moved to my shoulder, feeling the shape and sharpness of the little bone within me that I had never thought of before. The last was a fracture line, drawn with astonishing straightness across the length of where my arm joins my shoulder.

I should have learned then: Never turn your back on the ocean. Even when the crown of your head breaks the surface and your limbs find their footing, the deluge can still overtake you. It will pull you to its dark bed, ravage you, leave you gasping for air and broken.

* * *

Within ten days I flew home to Windsor, Pete having left before me on his pre-booked flight. My mother and sister met me when I landed at the airport, my arm in a sling. Ontario was in deep winter. I met with an orthopaedic surgeon who recommended six weeks in a sling before beginning re-habilitation. I took comfort in spending time with friends and family and in the many small luxuries of home. At night, I slept in a large cushy recliner in the living room to avoid putting pressure on my arm.

Several weeks later, while asleep in the chair, I woke in the night with chest pain so severe that I thought I was having a heart attack. It didn't subside. At the emergency room, the EKG came back normal and the doctor pre-scribed a drug for heartburn, though I had never before had heartburn. I had also recently noticed a lump under my left arm and took the chance to ask the doctor about it.

"If it's not gone in a week, go see your family doctor," he said.

The lump was painless and firm and didn't go away. My family doctor booked me for an ultrasound, which led to a CT scan and then to a biopsy.

If this series of tests happened now, I would *know*. But because I had never travelled this road, I could not see where the signs were leading. Signs like the night I had gone to bed with a hot water bottle and woken up, drenched. Thinking the bottle's seal had broken I got up to change, only to see in the light that it was intact. I had been sweating so much that my clothes were wet. Another night, I woke with severe chills. I started pulling clothing off of my shelves, putting on layers of pants and shirts and even a toque. An hour later, I woke up drenched under the covers again. These extremes were the fevers that were attempting to kill the disease.

In the weeks it took to get these tests done, I had begun rehabilitation on my arm. The sling had come off and my arm was sore and weak. The therapy worked on increasing my range of motion and on building back some muscle mass. I returned to work teaching. Very quickly though, my mobility stopped progressing.

"I don't think it's a rehab problem," the therapist said. "I think it's a bone structure problem." She referred me back to the surgeon.

The day of the appointment, my mom woke up with a bad flu. I took the day off work and drove her to the clinic where our family doctors shared an office. After Mom was seen, we passed my doctor at his desk. I stopped and greeted him.

"Any results on that biopsy?" I asked. He ushered us into his office and pulled up the report on his computer.

"No one's contacted you? I'm so sorry, Anna. The biopsy came back as Hodgkin's lymphoma. It's cancer."

I don't remember those moments afterward, what I thought or said in return. I didn't feel devastated. That would come later. I don't remember feeling much at all. I still needed to get Mom home and attend the surgeon's appointment. I didn't particularly like the surgeon and felt he was arrogant. I was annoyed that months had passed and my arm had not greatly improved. Through another X-ray, he confirmed that my arm had not healed properly.

"Your arm," he said, "will need to be re-broken and fitted with a steel plate and screws."

"Well," I fired back, "I just found out that I have cancer and will be starting treatment next week." He leaned back in his chair, took his glasses off, set them down on the desk between us.

"*Who,*" he asked, "did you piss off?"

What could I say? Had I committed some unintended but grievous deed? Was this due to a series of errors and offences accumulated over my lifetime? And how could I not remember doing something so significant as to have given me *cancer*?

He told me to come back when my treatment was over and he'd do the surgery.

I didn't like him anyway. I never went back.

* * *

Twilight. That's what they called the anesthetic. Not a dawning, not a day, but an entry into night. Drugs that wouldn't render me unconscious but would bring me close to its shadows. It was the first surgery of my life; the implantation of a small device under the skin of my chest, meant to draw blood and deliver treatment. Lying on the table while the doctors and nurses prepped, I prepped too.

Deep breaths. Deep enough to get to the place inside of me that could never be anesthetized. *Body, we are about to be sent to a place of numbness. We won't be able to feel, but we'll know what's happening. We can trust and rest. I will be here, awake and vigilant.* Intake calm, discharge anxiety. Deep breaths.

I crouched inside, a candle, watching the surface above where my body was twilighted. The fluid was pushed in my arm. *It's okay sweet vein, open up, take it in.* I was submerged. The ceiling began to wobble, the tiles moving through jelly-cubed water.

I didn't feel the slit. I didn't feel the small hard disk moved under my skin like a boat into its slip. I felt nothing of the line threaded through my veins, routed towards my heart, and tethered to me. Only later did I see the anchor of stitches. A perfect blue bruise. How easy it is to add and subtract from your body.

This smooth circle — a *port*, it's called — docked into the right side of my chest, ready to take on saline and chemotherapy and transfusions, and to give back lines of blood. A ship meant to save my veins from waves of needles through storms of treatment. A tiny vessel to deliver life-saving cargo. I hovered in twilight, a stowaway on a ghostly sailing.

Port: a controlled haven; a safe harbour.

Why then, did I feel like I had just set out on an ocean of abyss?

2

Pause:
Temporary inaction;
To reconsider;
A brief suspension of the voice to indicate
the limits and relations of language.

Eleanor

Day 1

This British Columbian town is two ferry rides and five hours from the city and functions like an island. Though relatively small, it has its own hospital, airport and brewery. Modest homes are built on the slopes of the coastal mountains, so most people get an ocean view for cheap. Volkswagens and hybrids are driven by parents who more often wear dreads than suits. Locals make their own kombucha, sauerkraut and sweaters and the coffee is organic, fair-trade, shade-grown, bird-friendly and locally-roasted. Community events are *Waste Free! Wash Your Own Plate!* The graffiti reads *You are Be-You-To-Full* and *Trees are our elders.* It's a place where black bears, eagles and salmon are valued residents. There's multiple thrift stores and churches and a cannabis factory under construction. It's a friendly, welcoming place to live.

Our first time here was when Andrew and I came to visit my brother Sean, sister-in-law Ellen and their kids. They had made the move to the coast and sent pictures of themselves boating, gathering oysters and jumping off docks into lakes. They took us hiking on trails through Douglas firs, hemlock, spruce and cedar; giants in the old-growth forests that had escaped the area's logging activities. *Veterans,* these trees are called, some reaching hundreds of feet tall. The land was alive with warm, wet colour; red arbutus, blue cedar, pearl moss, slate rock, brown nut trees, orange skies at dusk. Hiking to the top of one of the mountains, we took in the view: The Pacific, dozens of lakes, sand beaches, forests and the coastal mountains. This place had it all.

We liked it so much that we got married here, moving the simple ceremony from the lakeside to the living room during a heavy rainstorm. We lit the wood stove and toasted Andrew's grandparents, who had also married in their living room. Our niece and nephew sat at our feet while we exchanged vows. Afterwards, Sean and Ellen got a babysitter and we went out for Thai food. Andrew and I wondered if we could move here. I had just begun a new treatment and it didn't seem possible. But a year-and-a-half later, the once-a-month drug seemed to be keeping the cancer in remission and we thought about the move again.

"Is it even possible?" I asked my doctor. "With all of my complications?" Within the week, she had made the referral — to one of the top lymphoma doctors in the country. He would see me in eight weeks. We packed what we could in the car, sold or stored the rest, and spent Thanksgiving with our families in Ontario.

We took ten days to drive the Trans-Canada Highway through the five provinces from Ontario to British Columbia. In Winnipeg, we stopped to visit the Human Rights Museum and listened to CBC radio as Justin Trudeau's Liberals won a majority government. We drove through prairie towns on our way to Tompkins, Saskatchewan where my grandmother was born. This part of my family's history is contained in fields of rusting farm machinery, dormant weather vanes and a few dusty roads. In Banff, after a breathtaking hike on a rugged trail, we bought over-priced sandwiches and watched the Blue Jays in the playoffs on our hotel room television.

A day before my appointment at the B.C. Cancer Agency, we arrived in Vancouver to the most traffic we'd seen since Ontario. We wound our way towards Stanley Park and there she was, the shining Pacific. Andrew and I were raised on the shores of the Great Lakes. Water is as necessary to our souls as it is to our cells. Smiling, we turned the car towards the coast, our sails to the wind.

* * *

It's raining lightly when I pull into the small parking lot this first morning, a change from the heat of the east. The hospital's free parking reveals something of the character of this community. The grounds are rimmed thick with blackberry bushes that prickle the toes of the evergreens. Today, clouds hover around the low building of only five stories. The hospital has space for medical essentials: blood labs and imaging machines, operating rooms, oncology, labour and delivery and psychiatric admissions. There is a 24-hour emergency room which often doubles as a walk-in clinic because of the area's lack of urgent care centres. Those awaiting major surgeries or with complex medical issues are sent to *The City* for treatment. This hospital has a reputation for good, friendly medical service.

Inside the automatic doors, I pump sanitizer into my hands. I follow the directions that Alex has given me: through the lobby, elevators to the 4th floor, turn right towards ACP, *Acute Care and Paediatrics*. After I introduce myself at the nurses' station, I'm told that Dani, the clerk who I'm to check in with, is away. There is no hospice name tag left for me. Instead, I'm pointed to the far end of a hallway, towards room 444.

I know a woman who works casual hours here. She's told me that ACP is a sort of catch-all floor, with patients who have undergone minor surgery to the very ill. Although 444 is the only room designated for hospice use, at any given time there may be others who are dying on this floor. The town's temperate weather, proximity to a major city and natural beauty has attracted many retirees. A quarter of the local citizens are over the age of 65, with this number rising every year. The few long-term care facilities in the area are strained with waiting lists. The hospice society here began two years ago and there is yet to be a residence solely for the dying. Those who can't be cared for by family or in a long-term care facility have no option but to come to the hospital to die.

I begin down the hall with the quick step of health. Then something of this place — the waxed floor or the fluorescent glare or maybe the stale air — rouses some petrified remains in me. My feet remember first. They slow, persuading my arms to loiter more heavily beside them. Breath takes its cue; nostrils lengthen their pull, lungs hold, then slowly release. I reach the room.

Something shifts. There is deep settling, met and matched by deep arising. Grounding and Arising. Two simultaneous movements of a single substance. This twin shifting allows me to become aware of myself, my way of being, and this space I am about to enter, given over for the dying. I hold in this moment a recognition of the person I am about to meet and of the relationship we are about to begin. There is a pause, pregnant with thanks and with blessings. This practice is so helpful in preparing me that it becomes the starting point for all consecutive visits. *Grounded in the pause*, I step inside.

The room is an upgrade from the others I've passed. Wood panelling, though dated, covers the lower half of the walls. There is a big window that looks west to a stand of massive Douglas firs, beyond which lies the ocean. The window is flanked on either side by dark wooden shelves. One unit is labelled *Personal Items* and has the disclaimer that *The hospital is not responsible for missing or lost items* and to *Please bring valuables home with you*. There are no personal items to go missing or lost on these shelves, valuable or otherwise. The other unit holds rows of movies, a variety of family-friendly blockbusters. They appear to never have been opened. Between these shelves, under the window, is a sofa made of a wipeable synthetic material. It looks as though it converts to a yet-to-be-pulled-out pullout bed. In the opposite corner, there is a private bathroom.

There are a few pictures on the wall, mostly Zen-inspired flower scenes. Several have small brass plaques mounted beneath them, inscribed with names that follow *Donated in memory of* or *In honour of.* There's a large bulletin board too, similar to the one in the isolation room where I lived for a month. I created a collage on it, taping positive quotes and notes from home around pictures of my friends and family. Tacked to this one is a TV channel guide. The other two dozen multicoloured pin faces float in empty space, looking for something to anchor.

Next to this hangs a white board with several headings ready for daily updates:

> *Today's date is:*
> *Your doctor is:*
> *Your nurse today is:*

These three are filled in. The last heading, *Expected discharge date,* is not.

Extending out from the wall closest to the window is a single bed. The bed has wheels that can spin in any direction or lock in place when necessary. It has multiple buttons to move the head or feet into a variety of heights and angles. The bed would seem to allow for a high degree of freedom if not for the hard plastic side rails raised on either side.

And there, in the middle of this bed, in the centre of this room, at the end of the hallway in this town's hospital on the western shores of Canada, northern hemisphere, planet Earth, Eleanor Davis is asleep in a mound of blue. Her head, the only visible part of her, lies on a blue pillow. The shape of her body is almost indistinguishable under the gown, sheet and blanket of the same shade of bland.

She is facing away from me, towards the window, and seems deeply asleep. I move around the bed in order to see her. Eleanor's face is full and soft-looking. Wrinkles line the extra skin around her neck and create folds on her earlobes. Her hair is thick and grey and falls around her ears. She looks to be of average height and round in the middle, but not obese. There is an easy familiarity to her, the comfortable archetype of a grandmother or elder.

I move towards the sofa. As I sit, the cushions exhale a loud scrunching sound that cause Eleanor's eyes to open and work to fix on me. Horrified at waking this dying woman with my butt-scrunches, I immediately stand and go to her side.

"Hello Eleanor. My name is Anna. I'm a volunteer with hospice. Alex said you might like some company?"

"Hi Anna!" Eleanor chirps. She seems genuinely happy to see me.

The next thing she says is, "I've had diarrhea all night. All night. Oh God! And now, I'm so tired."

And there, in this first moment of our meeting, illness does what it does best — it cuts through all pretence. Obligations to etiquette or social convention are shattered. The state of Eleanor's health plunders the niceties that form most new relationships. She doesn't have much time and she knows it. And this, *had diarrhea all night*, is as good a hospice report as any other.

In the moment that follows, her pause becomes an invitation to me, the stranger who has come to watch her die. *Can you deal with that? Will you meet me here, in the raw immediacy of my life? Are you up for this?* I am, in fact, relieved. I did not know how long it would take. Eleanor has cleared the way for a different discourse between us.

I touch her arm lightly and say, "Yes, that must be exhausting." She raises a hand, sticks a finger in her nose, feels the small tube that's giving her air. She fumbles with it, finally grasps it and pulls it out.

"Is that bothering you?" I ask.

"Yes," she says. And then, "I'm ready to die." Her voice is certain, clear, at ease. There is longing in these words.

"Yes," I say again.

Her hands shake a little, her body seems agitated. Without the tube, she becomes breathless. I take her hand, holding it loosely enough to give her the choice to move it away.

"Your body is working hard, Eleanor. Rest if you need to."

After a few minutes, she settles, closing her eyes halfway. I ask her if I can help her put her oxygen back in. She nods. I pick up the thin plastic tube. It runs from a pump on the wall above the bed and I can feel the cool air on my fingers. I gently place the two prongs in her nostrils then bring the length of the hose behind her head. When I touch her hair, it is soft and clean, and for these small mercies, I give thanks. When I'm finished, the tube is lopsided and the prongs crooked in her nose. I've done it wrong, but am not sure how. She falls asleep.

I move back to the sofa and lower myself slowly to avoid its wheeze. It too, gently lets out its air. I've decided to stay an hour, and twenty minutes have already passed. I sit and begin to get to know Eleanor. She sleeps on her back, her arms by her side. Her eyelids flutter slightly, but her body is still and restful. Today, I am introduced to the Eleanor who sleeps peacefully, whose body is still and whose breath is an even *in-out, in-out.* I begin to breathe with her *in-out, in-out,* a simple practice that Alex taught us at one of our volunteer meetings. It's particularly helpful when a client is quiet or in pain or sleeping, or volunteer anxiety sets in about *what should I be doing?* I get to know this restful Eleanor so that I will recognize when it begins to change.

Eleanor is still asleep when I stand to leave. On my way to the elevators, a large picture hangs, leading to the other wing on the 4th floor. In the picture are two sets of hands, long brown fingers weaving together to create a cradle of sorts. The hand-cradle cups a gorgeous wet newborn. The picture leads to the paediatric and maternity ward. As Eleanor lays dying on one side of this building, new life is being birthed on the other.

3

Limit:
Something that bounds, restrains, or confines;
A determining feature in logic;
The utmost extent, exasperating or intolerable.

Year 1

For *someone like me*, the oncologist said — young, otherwise healthy, early stage — there is about a 90% cure rate from Hodgkin's lymphoma. Equipped with this statistic, I assumed the role of head cheerleader. I packed my desk at work, assuring my colleagues that I would see them soon. I started a blog full of test details, bible quotes and pictures of me smiling next to hanging bags of chemo. I genuinely believed in the war against cancer. I had been sent into battle and I was going to *do this!*

Outpatient treatments were held in the *Chemo Suite*, a bright, windowed room ringed with recliners. Volunteers brought around cookies and tea, magazines and warmed blankets. My mom or sister, or occasionally a friend, would accompany me for the two-and-a-half hours I was hooked up to a pump that delivered drugs. Chemotherapy targets fast-growing cells, like the several sizeable tumours that had grown under both of my arms. But the cells in my hair, intestines, and bone marrow multiply quickly too, which is why I could expect baldness, nausea and a compromised immune system.

Chemo is not the enemy, I told myself. *Cancer is the enemy.* But when I looked at the plastic tubes pumping toxins directly to my bloodstream, and in the days afterwards when fatigue crushed me and my body suffered a range of problems like shingles, nerve damage and infertility, I had my doubts.

Instead of being in the Chemo Suite where all the other patients sat, my first treatment was done in a private room. This allowed the nurses to carefully watch for any allergic reaction to the drugs and also it seemed, for any emotional ones. My two sisters Trish and Michelle, both pregnant, came with Mom and me. I sat down on the bed, while the three of them hovered around, all waiting for the nurse. When she arrived, the first thing she did was look from one sister's round belly to the other. "I'm sorry," she said, "you're both going to have to wait in the lounge area. The chemo can be toxic to fetuses." *What may take their babies' lives may save mine.*

I am the second eldest of six children. I was five when my twin brothers were born and they were like my babies. As I grew, I worried about things like getting the laundry done and making sure my siblings behaved themselves. Becoming a mother to a large family of my own had never been anything other than a certainty. I never consciously decided on it; it wasn't one of several options to consider. It simply *was.* How could I so thoroughly inhabit a life I had not yet lived? And how could the destruction of that life feel so total?

Just before the doctor and I shook hands a few weeks before, he told me that the toxicity of the chemotherapy would damage my eggs, making the possibility of having my own children unlikely. I was given the option of harvesting my eggs, a procedure that would require me to see a specialist two hours from home and delay the treatment for some weeks. *What kind of choice is this?* I thought. *My life or new life?* I had married and divorced in my 20s. I had cancer. I began treatment immediately.

What I didn't know about that handshake was that it was the beginning of the end of both my previous life and my imagined future one. It was the beginning of the end of assumptions, of entitlement, of plans. I was willing to compromise, to negotiate the terms of my hopes for life in exchange for life itself. *Fine, I won't have children as long as... No hair. Fatigue. Hospitalization. I can handle it all as long as...* As long as. But for all my willingness to bravely accept these in exchange for my life, illness does not work this way. Illness has its own terms, and *as long as* is not one of them. But though I knew nothing of it yet, life had things to teach me, and at the end of my old ways of being, new ones waited to be born.

My sisters left the room. The nurse gloved- and gowned-up. It was the first of many isolating moments, created by the necessity of these drugs for my survival and their potential to harm healthy people. Only my mom stayed, skin bare, mouth unmasked. She touched me, held my hand, kissed my cheek, unafraid of the ramifications or simply overridden by love. At the time, chemotherapy was simply the best option we had.

* * *

Two weeks later, my nephew was born. The first picture Connor and I shared was taken an hour into his life. He is in my lap, swaddled in blue and my embrace, his face a pink scrunch from the press of birth. I still have my hair; it's pulled into the last ponytail I would wear for four years. I am smiling so widely that my gums are showing. In the midst of many small deaths, Connor burst into this world with perfect life. In the picture, I cling to him and to this hope birthed with him.

Two months later, another picture of us, this time in black and white. We are both bald. I am again in the recliner, holding his body along the length of my arm, his head in my palm. We are facing each other, a look of intensity and love filling the small space between us.

The scrapbook I kept of these first six months of treatment is stark. All of the photos are in black and white, pressed onto black paper. Each two-page spread represents a month, little notes scribbled at the bottom of each page: *First chemo, port inserted, no mouth sores.* There are printouts of my blood work results and the emotional rating scale that measured my depression, pain, anxiety. Both scales fluctuate up and down. There are pictures of me in stages towards baldness: *short bob, mohawk, shaved head # 1.*

Beneath the picture of Connor and me are a few lines of a poem by Robert L. Lynn.

> For cancer is so limited —
> It cannot cripple love.
> It cannot shatter hope.
> It cannot corrode faith.
> It cannot eat away peace.
> It cannot quench the spirit.
> Can cancer conquer you?

I doubt it, for the strengths I see in you have nothing to do with cells and blood and muscle.

In those six months, my cells and blood and muscle underwent a trauma they had never before experienced. So too did my sense of peace and courage. But both my body and spirit surprised me with their ability to recover. In many ways, I began to understand new meanings of resurrection. My cells died off, only to regenerate again. My fears soared, then were relaxed and replaced by quiet collectedness.

I knew I was lucky. I thought a lot about the people I had met in South America and Africa. Though I had a life-threatening illness, I also had housing, comfort, food and medical care. I had people who loved me. This particular combination made me more fortunate than most of the people on this planet.

The six months passed quickly. Some of the predicted side effects like low blood counts, mild nausea and hair loss happened. Many did not. In November, my sister came with me to my last treatment. Three nurses surrounded us singing, *Happy Last Chemo Day To Yoooouuu.* They fastened a small pin engraved with a daffodil and the word SUR-VIVOR on it to my shirt.

Mom threw a surprise get-together with my closest friends. Over appetizers and desserts, we celebrated the success of the treatment and my having come through it with relative ease. A picture from that day shows us huddled on the couch, arms slung around one another, all of us looking at the camera and smiling.

* * *

"You've had a remarkable response." The radiologist inked a small circle under each of my arms and one near my sternum. I was lying on a bed being tattooed for follow-up radiation. He finished and helped me up.

"No detectable cancer. Relax and enjoy the holidays. I'll see you in January after your PET scan and we'll get started."

I did a fist pump in my mind. *I had won.*

4

Eleanor

Day 2

When I arrive, there is a lunch tray on the bedside table. It holds a variety of liquids — milk, tea, water, juice, jello, and a boxed vanilla shake with the word *Renal* printed on the side. All of them are full. The ice in the water has melted.

When I walk to the bed to see Eleanor, it looks like she is wearing caky, pale makeup on her skin, though every line still shows. The skin around her eyes is pearly, like skin that has been protected from sunlight by well-worn glasses. As I move to the bedrail, Eleanor wakes.

"Hi Eleanor, it's Anna from hospice," I say. I've decided that I will introduce myself each time that I visit, in case she has forgotten who I am and why I have come.

"Hi Anna!" she says. She reaches with one hand for the rail. Her fingers grasp the top of it and she tries to pull herself up. I offer to help and when she accepts, I press the button that moves the head of the bed so that she can rest in a sitting position.

"That's better," she says.

"Eleanor, I'm sorry, I should have asked you yesterday, but what do you prefer to be called? Mrs. Davis? Eleanor?"

"Oh, Eleanor is fine," she says. "Or Ellie." Her hand waves through the air. "You know, I've been in here well, three or four days now." A bell starts ringing loudly in the hall. "Those damned things go off all the time," she says. "It's a wonder anyone gets any rest in here." A nurse rushes by the door and the bell stops.

"Is it raining?" she asks. I tell her that no, it's just cloudy.

"We moved here seven or eight years ago. Gorgeous. We love it. But lots of rain. My husband Ralph was American, but settled here when he got a job as an industrial engineer. He died last year."

Eleanor is interrupted by a women whose shoes clack quickly into the room before stopping abruptly at the end of the bed. A hospital lanyard with an ID card hangs around her neck. She talks from Eleanor's feet.

"Hi Mrs. Davis, I'm the nutritionist. Did you eat lunch today?" I wonder how she's missed the cart of room-temperature drinks next to her.

When Eleanor answers that no, she hasn't eaten anything today, the nutritionist makes a brisk note on the clipboard she is carrying. Then, she looks up again and asks, "Are you feeling sad?"

Eleanor simply says, "Yes."

"Well," the nutritionist continues, "maybe we should get you something for that."

And what exactly, I wonder, will you get for her? What pill is recommended to sedate the process of detaching from the body, from every place, person and reality you have ever known and ever loved? What is the ideal antidote for this process? A quickening or a dulling? I have known the desire to quell pain, emotionally and spiritually. But to do so is to also stunt the power held in dying.

Every great spiritual tradition uses deep symbolism for the transformation that comes only through death itself. The exile in the desert and the promised land; self-emptying and enlightenment; the cross and resurrection. Our death comes in many small ways; the losing of hair or a job or a loved one. These many little deaths help us to prepare for the death of our bodies. What is needed is not sedation of our experiences, but the wisdom and guidance to integrate them into our lives. Bringing life to its fullness means making room for sadness with joy, disappointment and success, loss and gain. Each of us, including this woman at Eleanor's feet, will be asked to bear and to birth our dying.

I look at the lunch tray. There could be many reasons Eleanor hasn't eaten — the tray is too far from her, she doesn't like the selection, she has no help to manage the straws or simply, her body no longer needs nutrition. Eleanor is not asked why she hasn't eaten or why she feels sad. I wonder what box on the clipboard must be ticked before this woman moves on to the next patient. Though I believe her to be well-intentioned, I wonder if she talks of drugs for Eleanor's benefit or for her own.

She stands there, awkwardly. Neither Eleanor nor I say a word. Finally noticing the tray of drinks, she plucks the renal shake from the table and hands it to me.

"See if you can get her to drink this," she says to me, as if Eleanor has disappeared from the room. She might as well have, since this woman has entirely missed meeting Eleanor in any real way. She swivels on her heel and takes her leave.

I look at Eleanor, worried this woman has shaken her sense of calm. But Eleanor looks back at me, raises her eyebrows and says with a laugh, "Know what I'd like? An ice-cold beer."

Day 3

I set the mason jar down on the table next to the sofa. This morning before leaving home, I cut three tiger lilies and a red crocosmia from the yard. Opened and flattened facedown next to the jar is a *Daily Bread* prayer book. When I pick it up, the reading is for June 22nd, two days ago. I wonder if a hospital chaplain is visiting. Eleanor stirs and opens her eyes.

"Good morning Eleanor. It's Anna. How was your night?" I ask.

"Pretty good, I think."

"I brought you some flowers."

"Can you bring them closer?" she asks. "I'm blind in my right eye." I bring the jar up to her line of sight, a few inches from her face. Her eyes slide together as they focus on the stems.

"They're beautiful."

"Yes, I love these, though they don't last long," I say. "How are you sleeping in here?"

"Oh, fine. Except for those damned bells going off every other minute. I even ate breakfast today." There is a glint in her eye.

"Ah-ha," I laugh. "Retributive eating."

"Two bites is two bites. Whatever it takes." She winks at me with her good eye.

She and I will get along just fine.

Day 4

When I come into the room, everything is droopy; the window blinds are still drawn, the lilies slouch in the jar, Eleanor's eyes are half-closed. I bend to her and say,

"Hi Eleanor, it's Anna. How are you feeling?" She begins to talk right away.

"I'm scared. I'm going to drown. This is a deep lake. A dangerous lake. Many people have drowned here." She pauses. "You...you go in a second. To the bottom. You won't come back. It's...it's like this." She raises a finger and slowly spirals it like a whirlpool. Then, she drops her hand and falls into an agitated sleep.

I pull the chair up parallel to the bed and face her. I've brought a book to read but end up just sitting next to Eleanor, my hand resting loosely on her arm. I watch the subtle twitches of her body. I breathe in, trying to take some of the fear from her and return feelings of peace and safety on my exhale. *In-out. In-out.* The air in here — warm and dry — makes me sleepy. I yawn and yawn again, finally give in and close my eyes, too.

Time passes. *In-out. In-out.* I become aware of the connections joining Eleanor and me; a small patch of human skin and the air that keeps us both alive. My awareness draws back to the corner of the room, where I watch two human beings breathe together. *In-out. In-out.*

After awhile, Eleanor's foot gives a small kick and I open my eyes. When I move my fingers from her arm, I see they have left slight indents in her fleshy skin. I remember she has kidney failure and likely can't flush fluids from her body.

Downstairs in the lobby I stop at the hand sanitizer pump, stationed by the doors like a silent distress signal. On my way in, it informs me that I may carry something harmful to the sick. I sanitize to protect them. But when I leave, it's the reverse. I may have picked up something harmful to myself. Eleanor's touch, and touching Eleanor, comes with a caution for both of us.

With my health history, I know this makes good medical sense. But this brief, routine practice has become a boundary marker for me. It separates the sterile world of the hospital, with its streaky floors and florescent lights and stuffy air, from the rich earth and the sunshine and the moving wind. It is as if the lotion, when dispensed in my hands, turns the world from colour to monochrome and back again. It is a psychological transition point, where I am dispensed the luxury of forgetting, of being able-bodied and well, of being able to prevent illness from clinging to my body and infiltrating my personal, private and protected life. Temporarily, I am able to distance myself from the almost-certainty of my dying in a hospital bed like Eleanor's, rather than allow the reality of our mutual deaths to penetrate my pores.

As I press the alcohol foam onto my hands, I think of Mother Teresa cleaning the wounds of leprosy. I think of my mother, holding her child's bare hand while toxins rush into it. And, I think of fingers, moving between them the ashes of a father. The foam becomes an anointing, an invitation to remember the sacredness of life and death, poured out for all of us.

5

Wallow:
To devote oneself entirely, to become abundantly supplied;
A comfort behaviour in a state of degeneracy;
Becoming, or remaining, helpless.

Year 2

I took the radiologist's advice and booked tickets for Mom and I to fly to Saskatchewan for Christmas. My sister and brother-in-law were expecting a baby, their second. On Christmas Eve, my sister and I opened my brother-in-law's gift; matching running shirts. We had decided to train to-gether — me, post-treatment and her, post-baby — for a spring 10k in Ottawa. After the gifts, we melted cheese and chocolate for a fondue and toasted the newest member of the family, whomever they may be. It was a girl, it turned out, and she arrived Christmas day.

With a new baby for my sister and brother-in-law to tend to, I took up the task of walking their two dogs. The temperature dipped to -30 degrees Celsius and the snow was ever-fresh and deep. Winter on the Canadian prairies is breathtaking. The sun finds room to stretch herself across the flat earth, opened in wide swaths by the sharp mouths of harvesting machines. The dry icy air also makes breath-taking a little harder. Pulling my boots from deep drifts, my inhales came in shorter, sharper snippets. But after a few days, this slight difficulty in catching my breath didn't improve.

One side effect of a cancer diagnosis is latent paranoia. *For the rest of your life, you'll always have to wonder if any ache or cough or bump is cancer,* said one doctor. The ache, the cough, the bump, triggers paranoia into expression.

I announced to my mother and sister that I was going to the emergency room to ask for a chest X-ray. *And no,* I told them, *I do not want company.* The fear I was trying to suppress instead surfaced on their faces. It was the initial manifestation of heartbreak.

Fear is an accomplished sorcerer. My awareness of a simple shortened inhale was quickly harnessed and exploited. Fear conjured images of pain, extended suffering and death. It was why I had to go alone. My body could hardly contain my own fear. It could not hold another's.

The X-ray came back normal. We breathed a collective sigh of relief. Paranoia went back to its den and life went on. The focus returned to this new life among us. We celebrated New Year's Eve and New Year's Day, the start of the year when *all of this would be behind me.* Having had a great holiday, we flew home.

A month later, I waited in the office of the radiologist, ready to discuss the results of the PET scan I had just had and to set dates for follow-up radiation. The door opened and the radiologist walked in and when I looked up and saw his face, I knew. After the initial elation of the clear chest X-ray, I had begun having full-blown symptoms again. In the last several weeks, I had awoken in the night with coughing, fevers and night sweats. *Abundantly supplied.*

As I began to cry he said, "I am truly sorry." I believed him. There was just nothing further he could do for me. I later wondered if he had déjà vu in that moment, of five years before sitting with another Byrne and saying, *I'm so sorry. There's nothing more I can do.*

At home, I emailed Colleen, a friend who was a nurse practitioner on my oncology unit. I told her what had happened. *What now?* I pleaded with her to tell me. She did.

"I'm going to ask Dr. Marian to take you on as a patient. She's our expert. You're going to want her."

I would be preparing to undergo a stem cell transplant.

* * *

The first time I met Dr. Marian, she said this: "I've gone back and reviewed everything in your case. I sent your original biopsy sample to London and Toronto for analysis. I needed to find out why the chemo appeared to work so well but then relapse occurred so quickly. London and Toronto have concluded that the biopsy shows cells indicative of both Hodgkin's and non-Hodgkin's lymphoma. It's extremely rare. It looks like you were misdiagnosed at the beginning. I'm so sorry." She paused. Mom grabbed my hand.

"A better term for what you have is Grey Zone lymphoma, where more than one type of lymphoma cell is present. I've done some research but worldwide, there isn't much. There's one study with good outcomes. It's based on only 14 people, but it's the best we've got." *Fourteen people. Worldwide.*

"It's a strong regime. You'll be admitted to the hospital and the drugs will be administered over four days. If you respond okay to the first dose, I'll increase the strength by 20% each time for five cycles. It's once every three weeks, so that should get us to transplant." I rubbed my new dark fuzzy hair. *A wallowing movement.*

Dr. Marian leaned in from the wheeled-stool she had pulled up close to me. She took my free hand and looked me in the eyes. God, how I appreciated that.

"I'll do my best."

She always has.

* * *

I shaved my head again. Number Two.

I was nervous about spending four days in the hospital. I had never been to the cancer ward and I wondered what sorts of things I would see there. I wondered about practical things, too. Would I have space and privacy? What would I eat? Would I be bored or lonely? How would I feel after these drugs?

Cancer is an excellent educator in the act of surrendering. It provides concrete, experiential immersion into a thousand ways to abandon your illusions. The particular culture and time I was born into promoted autonomy and control over one's life. I alone, it taught, choose my relationships, if, when, and where I go to school, and my job; the general direction and specific details of my life's trajectory. The associated belief is that this autonomy and resulting choices become fundamentally *who I am.* All successes are possible and my responsibility. Likewise, failures become mine, signs of personal shortcomings or lack of effort.

I was faithful to expectation. In my 20s, I earned an undergraduate degree and teaching certificate, got married and bought a house, and began working. I expected my 30s to be a productive time, having built long-term relationships, a home, a career. Instead, my first marriage ended, I was diagnosed with a serious illness and I needed to stop working. My fertility, my appearance and my confidence in autonomy suffered. I no longer lived up to my culture's ambitions for me and there was little I could do to change that. The shattering of this worldview created incredible pain. These losses felt like the loss of my Self. *A state of becoming or remaining, helpless.*

Then, over time and in remaining faithful to this unfolding, I began to see that this helplessness wasn't the darkness I had believed it to be. Helplessness became an essential step in my reorientation to an identity well beyond fluctuating circumstances. This identity is an abiding authority; secure, durable and always accessible. With time, my losses matured into trust. I learned that I did not lose control. *I lost the illusion that I had control.* That became a gift.

And so my time on the cancer ward became a way of finding a new balance between self-governance and the willingness to let go. When I arrived the morning of admission, I was happy to find that, as it was my first round with these particular drugs, I had been given a private room close to the nurses' station. The walls were painted in warm colours with wood trim and there was a TV and a mini fridge. I unpacked my clothes into the drawers and set a pile of books, a journal and a few pictures on the side table. I had brought my father's rosary, strung with dark green beads, each imprinted with a tiny shamrock. More and more, I treasured small comforts over grander gestures.

For the duration of my stay, I was attached to an IV pole, six-feet in height and hung with multiple bags of fluids.

Its thin pliable arm connected directly to the port in my chest, pumping chemo, hydration fluids and anti-nausea medication on a continual basis. When standing, my hand was always on this pole, as if it were a conjoined twin. Too much distance between the pole and me, or tangling my feet in its wheeled legs, or forgetting to unplug it from the wall, meant a burst of pain as the tubes pulled taut on the needle buried in my chest.

To survive at the time, psychologically as much as physically, I made small daily choices, acts of reclamation. When I woke early in the morning, when the halls were still dark and quiet, I would make a hot drink in the visitors lounge then climb back into bed for reading and meditation. I established a walking schedule, rounding the halls for 15 minutes at a time, four times a day. Because of the pole and because of the drugs, my walks were slow and methodical. I came to know which corners held linen carts and where the hot blankets were stored. I came to know each picture that hung on the otherwise empty walls. Most were countryside paintings overlaid with uplifting quotes. I came to know which nurses perpetually hurried from room-to-room and which patients never left theirs.

I spent nearly 100 hours in the hospital during this particular stay, my first. In the coming years, I would spend a total of roughly 2000 hours in hospitals, the equivalent of a year of full-time work. Hospital stays are not only a residing but an acculturation, an immersion into a territory with its own geography, language, dress code and protocol.

During admission, the comfort of clothing is traded for shapeless gowns. Wrists are affixed with identity bands that have little to do with selfhood. These visitors, some of whom will use this as their dying space, are asked to surrender their shoes. It is a vulnerable thing, to be shoeless. Vulnerable to the gods of medicine, vulnerable on this holy ground.

Hospitals are washed-out worlds, landscapes in shades of porridge. A throwaway land of plastic wristbands and tubes, masks and gloves. Little is soft or soothing. It smells of nothing but itself, immediately recognizable but not completely identifiable. Faint disinfectant, vague but persistent; the powder of plastic gloves, dry white air. There is no fresh air. *There is no fresh air.* It tastes of saccharine, of artificiality and metallic residue. The pleasures of food and drink become blended-down replicas of the originals. It sounds of squeaky steps on shiny floors from those who are allowed shoes. It's the ding of elevator doors and things on wheels, the soft wheeze of pumps that lullaby inhabitants to sleep. Here, the senses are starved, there is nothing rich to chew on, to savour or delight in. Even flowers are cut and dying, arranged in unnatural positions. There is nothing wild here; nothing except cells and fear.

There is a world of complex language, words with long latin roots compressed into short, clipped terms. The behaviour of diseased cells are referred to as *aberrant, resistant, anti, adverse.* Chemotherapies are abbreviated to words like *ICE, CHOP, Red Devil.* Vocabulary is only part of the narrative. The understory is rich with nuance — the slight downturn of a doctor's head as they read your results, the inflection given to a word — all that is communicated in the encounter between the eyes of two human beings when one holds news of the other. If you want to understand what is really happening to you, if you know what questions to ask, if you want your best chance of survival, you must become (and quickly) fluent in this tongue.

However carefully chosen or habitually used these terms are, they are not benign. This language of the workings and wreckage of disease is burdened with meaning. We know what destruction looks like. We know aberrance and deviance. And for those who harbour disease, what are we to do? These words describe something *in us,* something that *is us,* that is our own cells, our own flesh and blood and something that we simply cannot remove on our own. Poison it, cut it out, burn it out, but by any means, *get it out.* And get it out we must, if we want to live.

But any force taken against our illness is taken against the rest of us too, physically and emotionally. We try to externalize something that we are hosting on a cellular level. If we are not able to get rid of the disease, we feel embarrassed at having our bodies break down, ugly and dying, and not even being able to do that in privacy. What splintering of identity this can cause — to hate our disease but want to save our body.

This living, breathing organism I call my body is both inherently beautiful and implicitly fragile. The same pattern that is playing out in me will play out in every other living thing. Life, then death. Aging, illness, death. These are not mistakes to be rectified, but part of the whole. We cannot marginalize parts of ourselves, even the ones we deem undesirable. It all belongs in our one messy and marvellous life.

6

Cinder:
A fragment, hot but without flame;
Partially burned;
Still combustible.

Dad

Instead of fragrance there will be a stench;
instead of a sash, a rope;
instead of well-dressed hair, baldness;
instead of fine clothing, sackcloth;
instead of beauty, branding

- Isaiah 3:24

Light. Dark. Earth. Sky. Plant. Animal. Male. Female. A ram in the thicket, sacrificed. A people, walking the wilderness, parched and prayerful. A boy with a sling. A whale's belly and a lion's den. Two planks, nailed into a crossroad.

As a little girl, I turned the pages of scripture, looking at the drawings coloured into kings and creation, slaves and doves, floods and fire, temples and tombs. There were stories of death, the disobedience of children, the destruction of holy sites. The people in the stories grieved these as a violation of sacredness.

As a girl, it seemed that two gestures often accompanied the people's great grief. One was *rending*; they pulled out their hair, ripped their clothing, wore coarse garments of black goat hair. The other was the use of ashes, poured over heads or heaped up in piles to lay in. I felt these should repulse me, but I was transfixed by the scope of their sadness.

* * *

My dad was the kind of dad who carried a briefcase, who did the lawn mowing, car maintenance, and leak-fixing. *Blue jobs*, Mom called them. He was almost 40 when my parents married and began their years of raising six children. Dad loved to drive. Saturdays when we were little, he piled us into the old van we owned and took us into the country, the AM radio playing and the cream from his coffee spilling into the console. We stopped at the bird sanctuary and at every roadside stand. *Gregarious*, I once heard someone say when describing him. His temper flared easily with the noise and chaos of those years. Age, his and ours, softened him.

In the year after his retirement at the age of 65, Dad's main occupation became puttering; around the kitchen, in the garden, and in his workshop out in the garage. He and Mom took their long-awaited trip to Ireland.

Then, over a series of months, Dad's voice grew increasingly hoarse. A series of minor tests by our family doctor produced no cause. Finally, Mom drove Dad to the hospital for an esophageal probe. Less than an hour after the appointment began, Mom called, frantic. The probe had been blocked from entering my sedated father's throat. The blockage was a tumour, pressing on his larynx.

Dad was given an emergency procedure in which a hole, called a stoma, was cut into the base of his neck between his collar bones. Dad's airway was rerouted from his mouth and nose to this opening, which directly brought air into his lungs. He was also referred to a larger hospital in London to undergo an operation that would remove the tumour and his diseased voice box. An incision would be made below one of his ears across to the other; literally, his neck would be sliced open. Dad would need to relearn how to speak.

When Mom and Dad came home after the emergency stoma surgery, we didn't speak much about what had happened. We were all in shock, no one more so than Dad. I was a then-healthy 23-year-old and comforting my parents wasn't something I had ever needed to do. We hugged more often and a little tighter though, which I hoped communicated something of what I felt.

On the day Mom and Dad left for London several weeks later, my siblings and I stood around them in the living room, their suitcases and our fears piled up around us. Before they left out the front door, down the steps, into the car and to the surgery that would forever change all of us, Dad pulled us one by one into his arms. When it was my turn, Dad hugged me tight and whispered into my ear: *Take care of one another.*

It was the last thing I heard him speak with his own voice.

* * *

The weeks when Dad was in London for surgery, Mom with him, were difficult at home. I had returned after four years away at university. Living together again, my siblings and I fought under the stress of Dad's illness and our differing ways of dealing with it. I externalized the stress, excessively cleaning and trying to keep our house calm and orderly while feeling inwardly chaotic. My stress manifested in anger as I struggled for some sense of control. I thought that if I could keep the house and yard tidy, maybe the rest of my life would sort itself out, too. There were many times when I did not heed Dad's last words to care for my siblings. I simply couldn't deal with the mess of it all.

When Dad came home, his throat was swollen with the long incision. He was tired and worn-looking. As the weeks went on, I noticed he was different in other ways, too. There was now a tentativeness that surrounded him, a reserve, like he had lost some of his nerve. Indeed, he had. Much of what he loved to do was either altered or given up altogether. He wore small neck bibs to stop the dust of carpentry and gardening from entering his stoma. Fishing boats were out of the question. Falling overboard meant certain drowning as water would directly enter his lungs though his stoma.

And too, losing the ability to easily speak was a blow to Dad's gregariousness. He learned to use a Servox, a device that, when pressed to the neck, vibrated his vocal cords and allowed him to talk in a mechanized tone. He tried to have fun with it, buzzing it at us when our backs were turned and he wanted our attention. Several months after his stoma surgery, we travelled to Ohio for my brother's wedding. As my brother and new sister-in-law took to the floor for their first dance together, we formed a circle around them, blow-ing bubbles as they moved together. Dad held the wand to his neck and blew soapy spheres with the rest of us.

But there were embarrassing and frightening times for him, too. The mechanical voice the Servox produced could be difficult to understand, especially on the phone, without facial expressions and lip reading. It drew a lot of unwanted attention in public.

Years later, Mom told me of a time when Dad had driven to Florida to visit his brother, something he had done for years. On the way, he stopped at a payphone to call my uncle. It was miles later when he realized he had forgotten his Servox in the booth. I imagine him careening the car back through a string of small towns, screeching up next to phone booths, thrusting his panicked hands through the doors in search of his voice.

A few months after the surgery, Dad began four weeks of daily radiation treatments. He posed with the mask the radiologists had crafted to protect his head while the beams of radiation were aimed at his neck. It looked like a prop from a scary movie. The radiation was fatiguing but afterwards, Dad started to regain both his strength and lightheartedness. Soon after, I got engaged. Dad took my hands in his and promised to be there to walk me down the aisle.

Dad got better.

7

Mask:
To cover or partially cover;
To protect;
To disguise.

Eleanor

Day 5

Eleanor is sitting in an upright position, her eyes open.

"Hi Anna!" she says when she sees me, and this small, happy recognition touches me.

"Hiya Eleanor, it's great to see you today. How are you?"

"I'm thirsty. I'm so thirsty."

I unwrap the plastic bendable straw attached to the box of shake and stick it in. I bring it to her lips and she drinks without breathing for a few seconds. Then she burps, and a thin line of shake comes from the edge of her mouth. I wipe it away and ask if she'd like more.

"Colder," she says, gasping a little. In the last few days, I've learned that cold drinks are a pleasure for Eleanor. She's always enjoyed them she tells me, but in the warm, dry hospital air, the icy shock has become a delight.

I walk to the opposite end of the ward where there is a lounge. Two men sit in wheelchairs watching what looks to be a soap opera. One of them glances up and I smile. On one of the tables, the border of a puzzle is laid out waiting to be completed. I turn to the kitchenette, where there is a microwave, toaster and a condiment container filled with little packages of coffee whitener, sweetener, ketchup, salt and pepper. I choose two plastic mauve-coloured cups from the tray marked *Clean Dishes* and push the machine's ice button to fill them. To one of them I add water, leaving the other for the nutritional shake. I head back to Eleanor's room.

Halfway down the hall ahead of me, a large woman wrapped in two gowns (one front, one back) slowly pushes a walker while a nurse holds her arm. I quickly outpace them and then must come up short to avoid running into them. I begin taking baby steps. The nurse finally notices me and steps aside to let me pass. Now I quicken my pace again. As I pass, the woman turns her head up towards me. I smile sheepishly.

I think of my IV pole on wheels, pushing it in excruciatingly slow circles around the nurse's station. A few times, I was so weak that Andrew had to push me in a wheelchair. All the while the healthy world continued its frenetic pace, glancing down sympathetically as it passed, too. Now, as my eyes meet this woman's, I remember myself in her. It is too easy to let energy, ease and ability become self-important impatience. It is too easy to forget.

I hand Eleanor the ice water. She quickly drinks all of it, coughs and asks for more. This time, after filling the glasses I try giving Eleanor sips, clamping down on the straw periodically so she doesn't choke. I wonder if she's thirsty or if her mouth is just dry from breathing through it all of the

43

time. In the hallway, the call bell goes off. Eleanor says, "I hate those bells. I'm going to smash them." She raises a fist. I get up and close the door, but a few minutes later, a nurse pushes it back open.

"It's time for your painkiller Mrs. Davis."

Eleanor protests. "In my stomach? No, not in my stomach."

"No, in your arm," the nurse says, pulling up her sleeve to reveal a spot for needles to slip into her upper arm.

"It will just sting for a minute." Eleanor grimaces but then it's over and the nurse leaves.

"Did you know I'm almost blind?" Eleanor asks me.

"Yes," I say, "I remember."

"Well, the blindness, it's in my hand, my right hand. No. No, my arm, it's in my arm." She is confused. She knows this isn't right, but can't seem to find the word.

"Your eye, Eleanor? It's in your right eye?"

"Yes," she says, "that's it. I'm blind in my right eye."

I tell her about the night before, when I took part in a meeting held in the basement of the church she attends. The meeting was an information session about supports for the refugee family who would soon be moving to town. I describe to her how, as I pulled into the parking lot, the light of the sinking sun had reached the restored wood and stained-glass windows, making them warm and golden.

I had pictured Eleanor arriving there on a Sunday morning, perhaps in black slacks and a blouse. I imagined her body taking the steps through the entrance, down the flight of stairs and into the nave. I held the thought that this woman, the one I know now as unable to walk or toilet herself, had for most of her years shaken hands, nodded, sung and spoken effortlessly. Thousands of subtleties taken for granted.

I know almost nothing about Eleanor. I know nothing of her personality as a baby, what food she likes, who her best friend was or if she enjoyed school. I don't know when her heart first opened to love, or the first time it broke, or the last time it broke, or if it was opening or breaking now.

Nor is there anyone to tell Eleanor's story. There is not a single living soul here who has known Eleanor for the duration of her life. There is no one sitting bedside to share Eleanor as a daughter, sister, aunt, wife, mother or friend. There are no photographs, no long-collected items of hobbies or interests, not even one piece of her own clothing. There is a total absence of the external identity that for so long helped to define Eleanor. In fact, Eleanor is able to assume more about me than I of her. But Eleanor doesn't seem to need to know more than what my presence communicates. She has no expectations for me to fill. She doesn't require me to remember her medication or change her clothes or bath her. She certainly does not ask about my degrees and achievements.

It's curious, the affinity I already feel for Eleanor. In some ways, this closeness has been facilitated by these absences. There is no navigating the subtleties of long relationships, no past hurts or unexpressed desires, no competing distresses of family members. We meet on this ground of being, where she and I can enter almost unobstructed from one another. In another place or time, our few hours together would serve as an introduction, moments in which the desire and capacity to begin a friendship would be decided. But here in this small room, what we are offered is raw presence, stripped-down to its simplest form. No one tells me what Eleanor has done with her time or what she dislikes or who Eleanor is to them. There is only Eleanor, *as she is*. She extends this same invitation to me, to be with her *as I am*. When I come into the room, she holds her hand up to me in silent trust. I grasp it in silent gratitude.

I tell Eleanor that it was my first visit to the church, that it was a beautiful place, that I had thought of her.

"Yes...thank you. It's...it's a beautiful church." She raises a hand towards me.

"Tomorrow I would like..." She gasps deeply, pauses, begins again.

"Tomorrow I would like..." Her hand drops.

"Tomorrow..."

Day 6

I sit on the couch and reach for my journal when Eleanor's eyes open, wide and wild. Her fingers motion outward from her mouth, a fist at her lips then splaying out and open. Her legs kick at the sheets trying to free themselves. She is going to vomit.

I jump up and press the call button. "Hang on Eleanor, I'm getting something." In the bathroom I find a teal kidney-shaped basin and run it back to the bed.

Once, while in the hospital, I was waiting to be discharged after a four-day admission for chemo. I was anxious to leave. Despite the anti-nausea medication I was taking, when I swung my legs to the side of the bed I knew I was going to be sick. I put my dizzy head between my legs and puked several times on the floor. I felt badly for my roommate who listened to the splatter hit the terrazzo. When my nurse came in afterwards she said, "Just a tip. If you ever have to vomit, do it on your blankets. It absorbs immediately and can be picked up and thrown into the laundry."

A nurse enters the room. Eleanor is hunched over the plastic kidney that looks too small to catch anything. The nurse checks her chart and apologizes. Eleanor's anti-nausea medication was only given five hours ago, and isn't due for another three. The only other option is a pill, which she can't swallow.

"Try to rest Mrs. Davis." The nurse eases Eleanor back into bed and pulls the covers up before she leaves. The wave of nausea passes, leaving Eleanor exhausted. She lays back and quickly falls asleep. I pull a clean washcloth from the supply cart in the hall and dampen it with cool water. I wipe Eleanor's face, ears and neck, then dampen it again and lay it across her forehead. I move to the side table looking for a mouth sponge. There is a small plastic case and I bend to it and peer inside. It has teeth in it. The label reads *Eleanor Madeline Davis. D.O.B.: April 24th, 1938.* Eleanor is 78. Her middle name is Madeline. This tiny denture case is like a cedar-lined memory chest, for the secrets it holds of Eleanor. I unwrap the small pink sponge on a stick and moisten it. When I place it along Eleanor's lips, she opens them like a rooting reflex. I wipe the inside of her mouth with the sponge, all while her eyes remain closed, the kidney bowl resting on her stomach.

Today, I sit with the aloneness of Eleanor's dying. How many times today has she felt like this? Even with my visits, for 23 hours of the day, she is alone. I feel the vulnerability that surrounds Eleanor, the absence of loved ones. Critical illness depletes a person. Medicine masks the enormous amount of energy the body requires to regulate itself in the midst of acute pain, wounding or a failing organ. Any available energy is diverted to survival. You are often too weak to meet your basic needs, let alone any comforts, never mind self-advocacy. A hospital admission can offer a measure of physical and emotional stability, but it cannot fully alleviate psychological vulnerability.

There is a loneliness to being sick. No one can be sick *with* you, not really. You are the one who lies alone in the rough-sheeted bed at night. You are the one whose hallmarks of illness are highlighted by florescent lights and whose dreams are penetrated by never-stop-ringing alarms. You are the one to endure the itch of your cheek because exhaustion won't allow your hand to lift and scratch. You are the patient, dependent on a small red button when vomiting or shitting or choking; the one reliant on the quick and compassionate response of others, literally for survival. And too, you are the one who will never again be able to blithely sermonize, *Well, everyone dies someday.*

Only love tempers this isolation. For many seasons, the worst of my physical and emotional afflictions were redeemed through loving contact with others. I told my mother not to fuss; she fussed anyway. A good chapstick, the nice-smelling lotion, food from home. It was talks with friends, the touch of my siblings — and silent presence — that made sickness bearable for so long. The mystery of anguish is that when shared, it does not multiply. Instead, it divides itself, becomes soothed and eased. When another cannot help but hold your suffering within themselves, *as their suffering*, anguish crystallizes into a deep unbreakable love. It was and always is, the simple things, the things of love, that makes a life liveable.

My worst suffering comes when I see the thin sheath of skin around my body as a quarantine. When I believe that the breakdown of this body will mean the loss of me, while those I love remain alive, I am broken by a sense, of total aloneness. Fear is a frozen landscape that paralyses those who walk it and attempts to freeze our memory of the true ground from which we rise.

This is the Ground of Being[1] that births me again and again. Warmth and light steam up from it, evaporating fear and returning me to my place of belonging. At every step I have taken in life, this Ground has risen to meet me. This Ground holds me and joins me to all, endlessly and effortlessly.

This Ground is patterned by circles, the never-ending cycle of creating, rising, living, declining and dying that rings through everything. Stars, grass, insects, mountains — share this pattern. Dying is universal, necessary and perhaps, even good.

But shared dying isn't the solace of the Ground. An essential ingredient of the Ground is that nothing — not the stars, the grass, the insects, the mountain, nor me — actually ends. Our bodies are built from remnants of burst stars. The grass feeds the insect until the insect returns to the grass to grow the grass again. The mountain meets the rain and slowly slides away, only to be rebuilt when the creases of the earth converge again. All the while I am healthy and young or ill and aging, this cycle patterns time and matter and human hearts.

This template of re-creation is true not only for material reality but for inner transformation. Each time I feel I have arrived at some immovable understanding, I am

---

[1] Paul Tillich

brought — often by failing or fault — to a new, deeper, kinder way of knowing.

It is here that I can rest — having faith in the unfolding — though my skin will fall apart and away. Most times, with my limitations of thought and habitual emotions, it is difficult to remember this Ground. I am trying every day to live here, more and more.

Eleanor and I don't share the mutuality of years, but we arise from, and reside in, the same Ground of Being that bears everything from ancient times until the end. When I look at Eleanor, her life and death unfolding before me, what I see are my own.

8

Dormant:
Marked by a temporary suspension of activity;
Resting faculties;
Capable of being activated.

Year 2

Twice in my life, I have felt death try to secure itself in my body. The first came shortly after my initial hospital admission.

Usually, I didn't feel the effects of chemotherapy until a few days after treatment finished, when my cells began to die. I had tolerated the first outpatient chemo well. I lost my hair and had some fatigue but avoided severe nausea and infection. I continued most of my day-to-day activities with the exception of working and visiting crowded places.

Even this first four-day hospital admission passed quickly. I felt strong going into it, having had two months to recover from the previous drugs. Lots of visitors helped to fill the time. By discharge, I was a little tired and a little pale, but overall felt reasonably well.

It was February, a time of hibernation in Ontario. I took its cues of quiet stillness and long sleeps, spending hours in the recliner by the window reading, napping or looking out into winter's face. After a few days, Mom and I arranged for a good friend of ours, an elderly priest, to come for lunch. But by late-morning the day of the lunch, he called to reschedule. The blizzard had come quickly, the storm wrapping the sky in a dark blanket and tossing the ground into wild grey snow. I watched its approach, moving across the sky as it pulled the crisp blue-white dazzle of winter into a somber dream. It was the last thing I remember before the blackness came.

I began to vomit and couldn't stop. Mom somehow got me to the couch. Over the next few hours, I alternated between vomiting and sleeping, my mother running the stainless-steel bowl to the bathroom to empty and rinse.

The phone rang. I began talking incoherently, mumbling and gesturing, desperate to express something impossibly tangled. I was in some state between consciousnesses. Later, I learned that Mom had pulled down my pants and inserted a prescription anti-nausea pill into my rectum. I kept throwing up.

Twilight came early. Snow had quickly covered the long driveway that connected our acre of land to the nearby highway. Mom, worried we'd be snowed-in, called an ambulance. I was immediately brought into the emergency room, but the doctors could not wake me. My clothes were removed and a catheter inserted into my bladder. I was moved to a steel table under an X-ray machine, placed over my chest for pictures. All of this I found out later from other people.

I awoke the next morning in a hospital gown, lying in a bed on a four-person ward, a needle in the skin of my hand. My mother and sister stood beside me. I looked around, my mind palming over the edges of this riddle, trying to click its pieces into place. Milky bits appeared — the recliner, red flashes in heavy snow, a stainless-steel glint, a muddle of words. Nothing of the night. I began to cry cold amnesic tears.

I know a little of biology. The small structures of my cells that create my life force also house death. I know this continued cell death is necessary for the regeneration of cell life. But some seed of death had escaped its thin membrane and proliferated hungrily throughout my body, pushing up against my skin as it filled me. It crept into my mouth. I tasted it, this death. My death. I had been alive on this planet but had no recollection of it. I was both fascinated and terrified that my body could endure trauma to this degree while hiding it from my awareness. Such is the protective power of the body and mind.

For all of my efforts at rational thinking and conscious engagement in my illness, when my body needed to, it took over. I've known people who've survived cancer diagnoses heaped onto bodies already afflicted with diabetes, obesity or heart problems. The body is resilient. I've known others, young and strong and healthy, who have succumbed to microscopic bacteria. The body is fragile.

My body had gone somewhere without me. This living, breathing organism that I reside in had taken passage to a place in which I could not consciously accompany it. It was the mystery of being somewhere while simultaneous not being there, of being rooted in a body while being absent from it at the same time. I was knocked unconscious by the sail of my own lifeboat while it turned and carried me in another direction. Now, recognizing this fragile strength of my body, every cell in me let down and cried.

My sister had driven through the storm to the hospital, after hearing Mom's voice on the phone call. I realized that she likely was there when my clothes were stripped off and the catheter inserted. Weeks later, I got up my nerve to ask her about it. *What can you tell me about that night? What do you remember? What can you tell me about my life and death?*

She shook her head. "It was bad." She never told me more. No cause was ever found. The most likely was a combination of pressure on my heart, brought on by the chemotherapy and severe dehydration from vomiting.

I do not know what had happened to my body that night, nor what helped it in the end, but I do understand that the circumstances could have gone another way. I came to know a little more of death; its contours that are at once sharp but shapeless, the way it refuses to openly declare itself though so firmly occupying its territory.

My work became to trust that my body did not and would not betray me. This episode, this cancer, this eventual death is not an abandonment or an error, but an inherent part of its design. The body has collapse programmed into its core and the body will remain faithful to carrying out this end. I am asked to do the same; to host and facilitate the conversation that is always occurring between my life and its certain end and to reconcile myself with both its enduring and ending parts. If I can do this with as much openness and sincerity as I am able, this fragility and strength, this illness and aliveness, the scent and taste of death and life, somehow makes the world more beautiful.

* * *

A few weeks later, March arrived. My blood counts recovered enough that Dr. Marian decided to go ahead with the dose increase. To ease our concern about another reaction, she arranged for a home care nurse to visit after I was discharged. This second time around, the regime exhausted me.

This exhaustion is something that *tiredness* does not begin to touch. Going home after hospital stays, I wanted to do as much as I could for myself to ease the reliance I had on my mom for most of my treatments. I wanted her to be able to rest and to have her own life. After this second time around, I wasn't afforded the same choice.

Keeping my spine upright in order to hold up my head required too much energy. Showering was impossible. I could only lay listless in the tub, wiped-out by the heat. Afterwards, I would wrap a towel around me and then lay on the bed, damp and too tired to care. Dressing became a planned event. Sit down. Take off the shirt. Rest. Pull on another. Rest. Pants off. Rest. Pants on. Rest. One sock. Rest. Other sock. Nap. It was difficult to get up for a drink and making food was unimaginable. If I could have sent someone to the bathroom on my behalf, I would have.

I felt a little sick and completely depleted all the time. Nothing tasted right and my lack of eating made me weaker. Keeping my eyes open to watch a movie was too draining. Most of my hours, I lay on the couch enfolded in a haze, not really awake or asleep. I ran reels in my mind of how I had been just a few days before, people complaining about keeping pace with my long stride and high energy.

My 33rd birthday fell a few days after my second discharge. Three of my closest friends arranged a brunch at one of their homes. I got ready while sitting on the couch, slowly putting on a bit of makeup. I felt terrible that morning, exhausted and not the slightest bit hungry. Before I was due to leave, the home nurse stopped in to see how I was doing. I left the couch for the kitchen table, sitting up as she took my temperature. But it was too much for me and I said, "I'm sorry. I need to lie down." We all stood, the nurse and my mom immediately flanking me. I took a few steps.

When I came to, I was on my knees, my arms held up by them on either side. They slowly lowered me to the hardwood and slid a pillow under my head. The nurse took my blood pressure.

"82/52,"she said, pulling at her stethoscope earbuds. "No wonder you feel terrible. I think you need hydration." I groaned. It was my *birthday.*

"It won't take long, but it will make you feel a whole lot better." Humility pulled up in the ambulance. The nurse asked the attendants to carry me out of the house. *At least I did my makeup,* I thought, embarrassed. She was right though. I was quickly given a bed in the emergency room, hooked to hydration, and soon left feeling much better.

Then, within a week, my body passed the majority of toxins from my system. Almost as quickly as it had come, the fatigue began to disappear. I began eating, then walking, then generally just feeling better. How quickly and completely this exhaustion occurred always surprised me. Later, I grew to know this rhythm, the week of all-out exhaustion whose ending is unfathomable, followed by its sudden recession as my blood counts recovered. It was always surprising, this fragility and strength.

My family held a birthday dinner for me. I sat upright at the table, a plastic crown atop my bald head and my four-year-old niece in my lap. When Mom brought out the cake I paused, letting my face be illuminated by the flames of the years of my life. It was my first birthday with cancer. I closed my eyes, took a breath deep with intention, and blew out what would become my yearly mantra. *I wish for another year of life.*

9

Witness:
To observe, to watch;
To serve as evidence of;
An open profession of faith.

Eleanor

Day 7

When I come in mid-morning, Eleanor is sitting up in bed, her eyes partly open. I take her hand and bend close to her face.

"Good morning Eleanor. It's Anna. Do you want the bed down?" Eleanor opens her eyes a little wider and slowly says, "The nurse. Is going. To wash me."

"Ok," I tell her. Her eyes drift closed. I stand by the bed, slightly crouched over so I can keep holding her hand.

Soon, a nurse with short, tightly-curled hair comes in with a stack of clean items: sheets, a gown, facecloths and towels.

"I'll be back," she says, placing them by Eleanor's feet.

There are a few quiet minutes and then Eleanor begins to groan. The sounds are weak and distant at first, coming from somewhere far-off as she sleeps. But soon, the groans get louder and worsen as if she's in pain. She begins to rub her stomach, then wakes.

"I need to poo. Oh, I need to poo! I can't wait!" I reach down and press the nurses' call button.

"Ok Eleanor, the nurse is coming. It'll be just a minute. Are you wearing something?" I ask, meaning disposable briefs.

"Yes," Eleanor moans.

"Ok then, go if you need to, but a nurse is on the way." I hope this is true.

The urgency in her bowels gives Eleanor a burst of adrenaline. She manages to pull herself up and onto the edge of the bed using the side rails. Her legs dangle. I'm afraid she's going to try to stand up. I don't think I'll be able to support her, but I also can't hold her down. I keep talking.

"The nurse will be here anytime to help you. I'm going to stay with you." A few minutes go by as Eleanor continues to groan. Finally, a nurse with a thick Irish accent arrives. He goes right to Eleanor.

"How're you doing, darling?" he asks. "I haven't seen you in awhile."

Eleanor turns her face upward to him and says, "I need to poo." He bends and wraps her in a big hug.

"No problem, Love." I like him instantly. A second nurse pushes in a commode then runs back to the hallway for a clean pan to slide underneath. When she returns the nurse says, "Dance with me, Eleanor." He threads his arms under hers, lifts her to her feet, and gently swings her around onto the commode.

"You're a wonderful dancer!" he tells Eleanor.

I excuse myself and as I step into the hall, the second nurse closes the door behind me. I walk towards the end of the corridor where it's quiet. There are two more rooms and an office, all of which are empty. The office is a glassed-in cubicle. I bend to read the poster on the door:

<u>TEAM</u>

Together
Everyone
Achieves
More

A few doors down in the other direction there is an out-of-the-way door that reads *Staff Only*. I stop next to it and lean against the wall to wait. A man wearing a blue gown with brown plaid pyjama pants underneath shuffles towards me then stops.

"You really afraid someone might try to go through there?" he asks.

I look at him, confused, then realize that despite my jeans, t-shirt and casual leaning, he thinks I'm security. This is how subtle the power imbalance is in medical facilities. Something about my youth, my stance, having my own clothing, confers some authority.

I tell him that no, I'm just waiting to visit a friend.

"Oh," he says. "Well, I wouldn't try going through there."

"Nope, wouldn't want to do that." I smile. He looks up at the *Staff Only* sign and then back at me before shuffling off.

I walk back towards room 444 and stop outside of the door. I can still hear groaning. The door is now slightly open and when I look in I see only Eleanor, hunched forward still sitting on the commode. Even from the crack in the door the smell is terrible; the sour contents of Eleanor's bowels that have left her body for open air. Clearly, Eleanor has had her poo.

I wait. No one returns. Eleanor is sitting there — just sitting there — bent over and groaning. What do I do? It seems wrong to wait, to not offer help as she sits, soiled. It's clear from her position that her previous energy burst is gone. She is too tired to get off of the commode herself and maybe too weak to press the call button. I can't imagine what the smell must be like in there. Do I go to the nurses' station? Go in and stay with her? Continue waiting?

Finally the image of Eleanor slumped over a pan of her faeces, and the increasing foul smell, makes my decision. I take a deep breath, hold it, push open the door and cross the room. Eleanor looks asleep. With no fan and no window that opens, the room stinks of stagnant diarrhea. I press the call button and say on an exhale, "The nurse is coming, Eleanor."

Then, I back out of the room.

It still takes several minutes of the near-screeching bell for the female nurse to arrive, this time alone. She grabs a fresh pair of gloves from the box affixed to the wall outside of Eleanor's room.

"I'm also going to wash her up now," she says to me, closing the door behind her.

I'm left standing in the hall again. I cross my arms, shift from my left foot to my right. I wonder how long the washing-up will take. Eleanor's need to go to the bathroom has taken the better part of 45 minutes. Guilt is already washing over me. I crack the door slightly and stick my head into the room.

"Maybe I'll just go now," I say, but Eleanor and the nurse are in the bathroom together and don't hear me. I grab my bag from the sofa and walk to the elevators. I pump sanitizer onto my hands while I wait for the doors to open. In the lobby, I use the public bathroom to scrub my hands, wrists, and forearms. I press the sanitizer one more time at the front doors. Out on the sidewalk I breathe as deeply as I can, trying to appease my senses. In my mind, I am doubled over, heaving out the smells.

I leave the hospital grounds and cross the road towards the mouth of the forest that Eleanor sees from her window. I step onto the trail that winds along a stream for several kilometres before exiting out onto the main street of town.

The woods are still under the domain of morning, cool and quiet, the scent of moss and pine on the breeze. The sun plays with the tree limbs to make shadow puppets on the path. I turn towards the creek and realize how quickly I have been walking. It takes a moment, an effort, for me to slow.

Footfall. Breathe.

Footfall. Breathe.

Walking. *W-awe-king*, I call it. *A devotional act that feeds the inner and outer self.* When my feet drop kisses on the earth's cheek, it responds in-kind by sending soft ripples of equanimity and joy through my body. I marvel at my ability to walk on this spinning sphere while it whirls through space.

Footfall. Breathe.

Footfall. Breathe.

My walks are acts of consuming. I am in love with this world. My lungs work to find new depths in which to pull in and hold something so much bigger than themselves. It is an attempt at unity with something incarnate in the bark and bugs and sky, and yet so unfathomable that I can only take big gulps at it.

But these forests cannot be consumed. British Columbia has some of the largest trees on the planet, a community of enormous, living entities that grow, sway, breathe and harbour innumerable living things. They are the tie rods that anchor the earth and exhale to the sky. When I disappear into their thick underbelly, it is I who am consumed.

Trees were the first to teach me to focus on the breath. As a child, I anticipated the arrival of our Christmas tree — *a real tree* — in our living room. Over the years, under the tutelage of trees, I began to learn about the breath. I learned that what I breathed in and out and what trees breathed in and out were exact opposites and miraculously, just what the other needed to survive.

I also began to understand that a tree's most fragrant time is when it begins to die. After a few weeks of living indoors, taking water from a dish and bringing joy reliant on its certain death, our Christmas tree seemed to take a long inhale. Then, with dried boughs laden with loosened needles, it breathed out its spirit, heavy with scent. It was an invitation to my child lungs. I breathed in this gift as deeply as I could, holding the fragrance in my nose, then letting out long and slow. Over and over, in and out, the tree and I breathed together. And so I learned to pay attention, and I learned the sweet scent of death.

As I grew older, my breathing became instructed by walking in nature, the slow measured breaths of plant life. Plants are the respiratory system of the earth, reminding us that this planet is alive. What would the breath of one million trees on a mountainside sound like? Deep, rhythmic, self-possessed. Babies breathe like this, and sages.

Footfall. Breathe.

Footfall. Breathe.

It is here, under the protection of these masters, the fir and cedar and pine, that I get honest. When Eleanor first moaned with cramps I was calm, focused. *It's okay Eleanor. The nurse will be here. I will stay with you.* By the time I left the hospital I felt anxious and guilty. *Eleanor needs privacy. She will be exhausted and need to rest. I am intruding.* But I begin to understand, as I gulp endlessly at the morning air, that my own limitations — not Eleanor's — have caused me to break witness with her. How did I so quickly move from groundedness to anxious rationalization?

From the first morning I met Eleanor when I took a moment of quiet outside of her door, a quality of being within me, and between Eleanor and me, has shown itself. When the doors of the hospital slide open, it is as if I am entering a realm understood only by the true and present Anna who has willingly brought herself to such a place. Despite initial impressions, there is an understated grace here, a tenderness, a soft beauty. When I choose this way of seeing and of being, the hospital becomes the ground for transformation, a monastery of devotion. My practice of centring allows me to understand this, to enter into it with more and more frequency.

But for my ego, this is completely destabilizing. My usual ways of being in the world, informed since birth and instructed in achieving, are confused by my conscious decision to place myself among the dying. It instead prefers activities that affirm wellbeing, esteem, pleasure and recreation. It is the primary driver when I care about how I dress, feel anxious about money, am hurt by the comments of others, and avoid unpleasant circumstances. It is the voice that tells me to skip visits with Eleanor in order to get more done. Taking this moment of grounding helps my ego to loosen a little.

But as I left Eleanor's room today and began to wander the halls, my mind wandered, too. I checked the clock. I thought about my lists. I began to doubt and my ego regained its footing. It's normal to have a physiological response to smells and sights like a bowel movement. Bodily functions — both Eleanor's and mine — are not inherently bad or good, they just *are*. But what happened in that moment was that they were *assigned* a value. I felt disgust at Eleanor's normal functions and shame at my sensory response.

When I anticipated meeting Eleanor, I thought I would feel nervous, but our time together has been relaxed and natural. There have been many moments during my visits with Eleanor, and in between them, that I have felt deep gratitude at being welcomed into her life. Now, with her body's vulnerability, my ego has betrayed my ability to witness all the ways of her dying.

Footfall. Breathe.

Footfall. Breathe.

Into this rhythm I settle and this rhythm settles me. I am gathered into myself again.

He comes to me then, pops into my awareness as the answer to my doubt. He, the sweet, chubby boy born the month of my first chemotherapy. The boy who wore diapers for the almost-five-years of his life. His survival depended on the consistency of our love and on our willingness to share in his body's fundamental needs.

Every few hours, we took into our hands the soiled mess of our shared suffering; the fullness of his dependence and of our helplessness, the cries of his discomfort and of our sorrow. Still, we chose. We chose to bear this with him, to unfasten and lower it away, exchanging it for a cool cloth and loving attention to every soft crease. We slid beneath him something of comfort, an assurance of our dedication to him. Then we reaped the rewards of holding close his warm and settled being. Over and over, this tending of shared wounds. The taking off of suffering, the cleansing, the redressing. It was an act prompted by necessity but fulfilled by love. Over and over, we were gifted the patience and fidelity that sustained us.

The changing of diapers became a spiritual practice as much as a practical one. In the physical repetitiousness of care, love became incarnate. His cries became a call to prayer, an opportunity to show up and share in something greater than ourselves, a place where suffering was infused with Spirit. We were invited into a breadth and depth of mutuality found and fostered by our fidelity to the perpetual changing of diapers. The service became sacrament, the liturgy of touch, where our humanity met our healing and giver and receiver were no longer distinguishable. How I wish for a lifetime of changing his diapers.

I walk towards the place where the path meets the creek on a small flat edge, just wide enough to crouch on. This creek, this forested path and me, stand on the traditional land of a people who have inhabited this part of the world for over 4000 years. The water here is pebbled and gurgling. I have come here before. It is a place of healing.

On one of my first appointments at the B.C. Cancer Agency, I met with a counsellor to talk about the depression and anxiety I was struggling with. I expressed an interest in alternatives to medical healing. The counsellor was from a

First Nation's community in the Yukon. She knew an elder in the community where I lived and encouraged me to visit him. I did, driving the winding road 10 kilometres north of town on a rainy afternoon. I met Paul at the health centre, a glass and cedar structure built to align with the four main points of the compass.

When I sat down on a chair in his small office, he began with a story, speaking with the quiet, firm voice of someone who has earned his wisdom. He spoke of the abduction of children, their forced confinement to a school system meant to break them of all things *Indian*. The physical, sexual and psychological abuse did break many, leaving generations plagued by trauma. Much of his job, he told me, was helping his people to heal their sense of disembodiment from their traditional ways.

He told all of this in a slow, deep way, offering it to me in small amounts so that I could follow. He asked if any of the story had resonated with me. When I called to set up the appointment, I hadn't told him of my cancer; only that I was interested in healing. Now, I pulled from my bag the hand-drawn medicine wheel the counsellor had given me and began talking.

"I've had cancer on and off for years. I've taken every kind of conventional treatment and still, it returns. The pain of facing dying in my 30s has touched every part of me." I pointed to the four quadrants of physical, mental, spiritual and emotional wellbeing.

"My 30s were supposed to be a time when my schooling, work and relationships came together. I wanted a steady job, marriage, a house, kids. Instead, I stopped working, was divorced and my health declined. All of the things I have done and thought I was supposed to do — who am I without them? Who am I if I don't objectively add anything to society but am only sick and dying? And what if I get better and don't want to return to that way of life? Who will I be then?

And then, somewhere in the re-diagnoses, somewhere in the incurable, I started to wonder about healing. I learned to listen to myself, to trust myself, to love myself. I'm more *me* than ever before, but the cancer persists."

He simply said, "Yes." Then, very quietly, he spoke a word. *SohoØot.* A traditional ritual for healing.

"Go to the river to wash. The water is your medicine. Go early in the morning so the whole day begins with healing. Before you enter, ask the water for guidance, for strength and energy. Enter the water. Let it carry away all of the hurts, the worries, the negativity. Recognize the healing that the water brings. Ask it for help. When you are finished, don't dry off too quickly. Let the medicine stay on you. Before you leave, say a prayer of thanks." He raised his hands to the sky. "When the winter is cold, you can do this in a basin or in the shower. Only do it wholeheartedly. Remember the healing that is there."

For several months I had. I walked the sandy rim between the continent and the ocean to a place where the land cracks open with freshwater. Here, the ocean's broad palm stretches inward to enfold the slender wrist of a river. It is an estuary, a place where mountain water rushes seabound and is greeted by a tide of salt. In autumn, this river fills with salmon leaving the sea to spawn in the freshwater beds of their birth. It is a place that defies the either/ors of salt and fresh, earth and water. Instead it is a place of changing sediments, transition and passage. This rich mingling of sea and fresh water nutrients make estuaries among the most fertile habitats in the world. It is like my port, mixing blood, saline, medicine as a womb for life. Mystery lives here.

Upstream there is a spot where the water is alive with energy, spilling over rocks into a deep, cold pool. It is there that I would bend, cup the water in my palms and bring it to my face in small splashes. Then, with the river beading on my cold cheeks, I would fill a bottle to later pour into a clay washing bowl at home. Or, at times, I would add a few drops and a bough of cedar to my bathwater. After a few days I would return the remainder of the water to the same spot, raising my hands in thanks as Paul had taught.

Now, I crouch on the flat low edge. I ask for healing for Eleanor, in whatever form she needs it most. I ask for healing for myself and strength to do right by her. I bring the river's wet face to mine. Over and over, I pour it on my head, hold it to my eyes, let it run into my mouth. Blood rushes to my cheeks.

This freshwater makes room for salt and for my own limitations. Its fertility rises from its ability to integrate seemingly opposing forces. This water does not sterilize; it cleanses. I watch my sadness, my doubt, my own shortcomings wash downstream. The water dries on my skin during the walk home.

Tomorrow, I will see Eleanor.

10

Transplant:
To transfer (an organ or tissue) from one individual to another;
To be supplanted from a milieu of ailment or infirmity
to one of wholeness;
To be brought to a new place when another is outgrown.

Year 2

April. My five siblings, their spouses and kids, flew to
Ontario for Easter weekend. My siblings have remained
close, rare perhaps for a large family who inherited their
parents' wanderlust. We live in different places across North
America and with the arrival of children and careers, found
it increasingly difficult to get together.

Eighteen of us converged back to the house and
acre of land that had been the setting for so much of our
childhood. It was a sunny weekend, warm enough for short-
sleeves. My sibling's kids, seven of them under the age of
eight, dyed hard-boiled eggs to shades of pink, blue and yellow, then later ran the yard in happy search of them. The
earth released the crocus; robins tugged worms from the
grass. The kitchen smelled of coffee, brewed in large pots
while we sat at the table around plates heaped with pancakes
and eggs, or sandwich fixings, or fish and salads, devilled

eggs and fruit. At night, as we had done many times together, we pulled our chairs into a circle around a bonfire in the yard, my brothers playing guitar as we sang into the night.

On our last full day together, I asked a friend to come and take some photos of us. Our property was divided from the fields behind it by two aging barns, built for sheltering combines and tractors. We played there as children, searching the spidery corners for rusty tools and old newsprint stories. Long since in use, they were no longer safe for exploration, the roof loosened by time and decay.

We used the barns as the backdrop for the photos, lining ourselves in front of them, our arms slung over each other like the twisting vines that were ingesting the weathered wood. It was almost impossible to get a picture in which of all of us are looking at the camera. In most of them, we can't stop laughing; wisecracks and jostling fill the space between us.

There is one picture of just my siblings and me. With my head wrapped in a scarf that falls to my shoulders, I'm turned towards my older brother, whose mouth is a mid-sentence gap. One of my younger brothers, a twin, has his arm straight in the air, pointing to the sky. The eyes of the other twin are crossed, making the faces of my two sisters fall open in laughter.

When we later look through them there are no perfect stances; someone is always squinting or looking away. But what is laid plain is the easy familiarity and affection between us. We have a messy, tested love, just tender enough and gutsy enough to endure. That's the real picture.

* * *

The other background to these photos was set weeks before in the London, Ontario office of the transplant doctor. Mom had accompanied me on the two-hour drive and after friendly introductions with the doctor, we sat together as he began.

"I'm going to tell you everything that I know about this procedure, the preparation you'll need to do, what to expect during your admission, the follow-up and recovery."

"Great. Thank you," I nodded. He held up his hand to stop me from continuing.

"And then I will tell you that none of this applies to you. In my career, I've seen a handful of people with your complications. I can't tell you whether your chances of a cure are 50% or 10%."

"Also, you'll need to complete a...."

Sober: To be freed from the habitual intoxication of hope.

My complications. Weren't we still talking about survivorship? After all of my rallying, my cliché one-liners, my prayers and tears and suffering? *After all of this*, I could no longer just die from cancer, but from its treatments.

"Anna? Anna, part of what you'll need to complete is a Power of Attorney and Personal Care Directive. It's part of the admission package. It's a precaution and one that we suggest to everyone. Do you have a will? You may want to consider a will."

I thought about those spongey rubber balls we used to play with as kids, the ones that if you threw hard enough against the floor would bounce back up and hit the ceiling. Up and down. Up and down. I imagined this doctor's words like those balls, ping-ponging around inside my mother's mind, demolishing the groundwork of her life. Thoughts of newborns and little girls, and of children who outlive you, shattered to debris. *10%*. Ping. *Complications.* Pong. *No machines, Mom, unless there's hope.* Ping. *Have Father Des speak. Let the kids blow bubbles.* Pong. *Then travel, and give my money away.* Smash.

Cancer is an equation, a thousand unknown quantities coalescing into diagnosis and prognosis. Age. Gender. Type of cancer. Stage. Initial health. Co-morbidity. Country of birth. Time period in history. If I had been diagnosed in the five years previous, I likely would not be alive. Born in 2050, I may never even have had cancer. You influence the ones you can — rest, eating, moving, healing, breathing, joy, gratitude — and you let go of the rest.

In math terms, my mother was the invariable. She was the constant that never changed and never left. While all the others were added, taken away, manipulated or mixed into various forms, she remained. She was the anchored factor that allowed me to endure the mystery.

We called the family home for Easter.

My favourite picture from that long weekend is the one of my mother with her grandchildren. She is in the middle, holding my nephew who is crying. Another grandson sulks at having his picture taken. One granddaughter holds a plastic egg over another's head. The oldest is holding the newborn, neither looking at the camera. Finally, the last boy is a blur of flying hair and limbs, captured mid-flight as he bolts away from the group towards the camera lens. In the centre of the picture, seated on the ground — *grounded* — in the midst of the chaos and flying limbs and tears of children, sits my mother, laughing.

* * *

The wonder of stem cells is that they are undifferentiated. They are not yet eye cells or liver cells or hair cells, but are able to grow into specific, needed parts of the body. A stem cell transplant is a procedure where healthy cells are taken (*harvested* is the term) from either a patient's non-diseased bone marrow or from a donor. The patient's immune system is then wiped out by a regime of strong chemotherapy and possibly, full-body radiation. Once both the cancer and the immune system are destroyed, the stem cells are injected into the patient with the hope that they will grow, divide and rebuild the body with an immune system protective against cancer.

To test my own cells, I had a bone marrow biopsy, a procedure where a large, hollow needle was inserted into my hipbone and samples of fluid and tissue withdrawn. It hurt. I laid in the fetal position while the nurse froze the skin on my lower back. It is impossible to freeze the bone itself. The doctor slipped the needle into the spot and pressed down until it bumped against my hipbone. With pressure, the needle was pushed through the bone where it clamped on a piece of marrow and then withdrawn. It was difficult to keep my back straight and not pull away.

It took two tries before the nurse held out a vial to me. In it was a small piece of bone. A few minutes ago it had been deep inside of my hip and now here it was, a small splinter from my frame. *Ok*, I thought, *get to the lab and show them that the whole structure is healthy.*

The marrow tested negative, which meant that the cancer had not spread to my bones and that my own cells could be harvested for use. Using my own cells eliminated the risk of rejection associated with cell donation from another person.

In May, my regular treatments ended, leaving me a month before the transplant to recover and regain some strength. My hair began to grow again, soft and dark. At times, I was nervous about the transplant as it meant a longer admission in a hospital two hours from home. Mom would be living near the hospital in accommodations for family members. Uncertainty and unknowing were constant companions. Accepting this, actually relaxing into this, was difficult with my survival mechanisms in an almost-constant heightened state. I worked at letting go and trusting.

I also practiced doing things that I didn't think I could, like the daily pinching of a bit of flesh on my stomach before sticking a needle into it. I started this during treatment, injecting my body with a white blood cell growth-stimulator to kickstart my immune system. Before the transplant I took these injections in the stomach again, this time to stimulate my bone marrow to produce such an excess of stem cells that they would be forced into my bloodstream for easy harvesting. After the injections, I was hooked up to a machine that pulled blood out through my central line and separated it into three parts; red blood cells, white blood cells and plasma. The stem cells were then skimmed off into a bag, treated with a preservative and frozen until the time of transplant.

I packed my bags with essentials — comfortable pyjamas, my journal, books. Most of my time though, I would come to find out, would be spent lying down simply resting and breathing.

* * *

By the time I was admitted for the transplant, I felt rested from weeks off of the previous chemo and buoyed by the time spent with my family. The first few days after admission, the effects of chemo hadn't yet hit, so I resumed my walking schedule while I could, circling the halls for 15 minutes at a time outside of the ward. When my blood counts dropped, I would be confined to an isolation room until they came up again.

My walks were a solitary time. Everyone, patients and nurses, were living and working in closed units. The art that hung on the walls became my companions. I gave each a little time, taking long pauses in front of them, studying a swirl of paint or a smudge of colour. I feasted on them, each a palette of encouragement. They whispered to me. *There is always beauty.*

One day, several after my admission, I was returning to my room when a painting caught my eye. I had somehow missed it on my previous strolls, though it was almost directly outside of my room. In the picture, chubby cherubs rested on clouds, looking peaceful. I'd seen similar ones. Still, I stopped and admired the circles that gave the painting its enchantment; the roundness of cheeks, the dimpled knees and soft clouds, the whorls and halos of a sacred sphere. And there, underneath, a small inscription. *Geri-Lynn West, 1977 - 1997.* My heart went to my stomach. Geri-Lynn. Geri. *Geri.*

Geri was the natural beauty of our high school group, her beauty matched by her sense of humour. She and I called each other on mornings before school to make sure we'd both be on the bus and would save the other a seat. Then, in our last year of high school, Geri began having trouble swallowing. It turned out to be a tumour in her throat, which turned out to be cancer, which turned out to be incurable.

When a group of us went out for my 19th birthday, Geri was too ill to go. We stopped by to see her afterwards. There is a picture of us from that day, six girls, arms around each other and smiling. One of us is bald, but still, we didn't know. In our youth and innocence and health we couldn't know, not in any real way, that one of us had turned towards death. And how could we have known, young and innocent as we were, that it wouldn't be just *one of us?* And though we've grown and though our innocence largely left us when Geri did, we still feel the youth in our bones and have difficulty grasping these matters of life and death.

Yet, here was Geri's painting right in front of me. She had been for treatment in this same hospital two hours from our hometown. She had walked these halls, seen the same nursing faces around her, perhaps even slept in the same bed. Here she was, immortalized in this sacred sphere, witnessing my journey as I had witnessed hers. From the haloed rings of light, she whispered to me.

> *There is always beauty.*
> *I've saved you a seat, friend.*

11

Space:
A limited area in one, two or three dimensions;
The distance needed in order to feel comfortable;
The opportunity to assert and experience one's needs freely.

Eleanor

Day 8

It's mid-afternoon when I step into Eleanor's room. There is a woman sitting on the couch reading. She has short grey hair and is wearing a blue cotton vest, with a name tag pinned to it that I can't read. Eleanor is asleep. The woman looks up as I knock softly and introduce myself. Since I've been told that Eleanor has no close relatives, I ask her if she's also a visitor from hospice.

"Not anymore," she answers. She invites me to sit with her. I do and find out immediately that Peg is a talker. Peg is a friend from Eleanor's church, the Baptist one in town. It turns out that she has also been visiting Eleanor every day.

"I volunteer downstairs with the Red Cross and just pop up after my shift." Peg tells me that Eleanor has a nephew who lives in Manitoba. "Every three days or so, I call to give him an update. He won't come at this point."

She goes on: "Years ago, before there was a proper society, hospice services were coordinated by one of the nurses. We had this wing staffed with volunteers Monday to Friday, visiting patients and offering snacks to families.

"After awhile," Peg continues, "I decided to just do visits on my own terms, as the need arose. That's how I started visiting Eleanor. Oh — do you know where the hospice cupboard is?"

When I tell her that no, I wasn't aware that there was a hospice cupboard, she motions for me to follow her. Across the hall is a small utility room with a cupboard labelled *Hospice*. Inside are some plastic cups, a kettle, coffee carafe and platter. Above it in the drawer are teabags, instant soup mixes and a box of cookies.

Back in the room, I tell Peg that I can return later to visit, but she's already gathering her book, water bottle and drug store flyers. She bends really close to Eleanor, who is sleeping and says loudly,

"I'm going to go now Eleanor. Anna's here."
Eleanor's eyes startle awake.

"My mouth," she says. "My mouth is so dry."

From the side table Peg unwraps a sponge-pop, dips it into a glass of ice water and puts it into Eleanor's mouth, moving it around and across her tongue. She pulls it out then takes a small tube of lip moisturizer and applies it thickly around Eleanor's mouth. Peg keeps talking.

"The doctor has her on two meds now. One to help her sleep and one to help control her nausea." Although Eleanor looks pale today, she does seem to be groaning less. I thank her for taking the time to show me the cupboard and tell her that I hope to see her again.

"Oh," she says from the doorway, "if she asks, there's a beer at the nurses' station for her. The doctor asked her what she'd like to drink and she said, *Corona*. Doubt she'll have it, but it's there." With a small wave of her hand and a smile, Peg leaves.

For the next forty minutes, it's just Eleanor and me. I think about the beer at the nurses' station, how different it seems from the philosophy of the nutritionist. What harm does a beer do to someone on their deathbed? But then I wonder if Eleanor is an alcoholic. She does have renal failure and a love of beer.

It's quiet. Eleanor occasionally mutters. "Make sure to let the dog in. He's a bad dog but he doesn't mean any harm. Is that a dog? Is that a dog or a horse in the bed? If he comes in here, there will be a big mess on the counter." She moves her head from side-to-side and tries to raise her arms. I touch her shoulder gently and say, "It's okay, you're alright."

I notice a man pass in front of Eleanor's door a few times. He's carrying a small bag of plain potato chips and seems to keep looking in, but doesn't come to the door.

When I gather my stuff and head towards the door, I hear Eleanor speak one more time from behind me. "Ack! What's wrong with that lady's neck?"

Day 9

"I'm going to the hospital!" I call to Andrew as I head out the front door. Eleanor and I are beginning our second week together. I wasn't sure we'd make it this long.

Not knowing how much time we have together has accelerated our friendship. Eleanor and I have our routines.

I've slipped into calling her Ellie, which she seems to like. When I arrive, if she is awake, I greet her and pull up the chair to talk. If she's sleeping, I quietly sit and hold her arm or hand, or sometimes meditate. Our time together is focused on small things: straws and ice cubes, washcloths and mouth wipes, hand-holding and sharing smiles. I sit or stand, making slight changes to Ellie's position so she can be comfortable. Most of our time together is settled in a silence that seems substantive; weighted with the patience required to wait for whatever chooses to show itself.

Today I wonder, as I walk towards room 444, if I'll find her there. I know that one day I'll come in the front of the hospital, up the elevator, down the hall and to the door of 444 and Ellie won't be there. The bed will be empty or will hold someone else's body.

But as I peer around the corner for her feet, she's there, sitting on the side of the bed, legs hanging down and oxygen off. I'm shocked. She's been sleeping so much during our last few visits that I'm surprised at her energy. I crouch next to her and she slings her arm across my shoulder and leans heavily on me.

"Hi Ellie. What are you doing?"

"I'm suffocating. I've been here three days and there's not enough air. I need air." Suddenly, a siren begins to whine loudly from the bed. Almost immediately, a nurse rushes in and presses a button, silencing it.

"It's a bed alarm," the nurse says. "It actually should've gone off as soon as she sat up. Mrs. Davis, let's get your oxygen back on." She threads the oxygen tube around her ears and into her nose, then eases Ellie back into bed. "Try breathing through your nose, Mrs. Davis."

Just then, Peg walks in. It takes her only a moment.

"Can you please bring her morphine?" Peg says. The nurse leaves to bring the sedative and I quickly fill Peg in, though she seems to know by Ellie's laboured and anxious breathing what has happened.

"Ellie, breathe through your nose," she says. "Close your mouth and breath through your nose. There's lots of air." Then, to me, "She's always been a mouth-breather." The nurse returns and gives Ellie the morphine. Peg and I sit down next to each other on the sofa and wait for Ellie to drift to sleep.

"They need to keep on top of that," Peg says. "She's getting more anxious when she's awake. Whatever it takes."

"Were you by chance a nurse?" I ask.

"Twenty-five years working intensive care."

I nod. "Thought you might be. Good skills to have around here. How long have you and Ellie known each other?"

"Oh, seven or eight years, I suppose. She and her husband Ralph came to an introductory course at the church. Ralph died just over a year ago. They have a trailer up north of town. I've been going there twice a week to check phone messages. There's been a few from a friend in Alberta but she never leaves a number, so I don't know what to do about that. The rest, well, she's already left it all in the hands of a lawyer. She knew she had kidney disease and set it all up well in advance. The lawyer is paying all of her bills and will take care of everything when she dies."

"She has a quick wit," I say, thinking of the beer in the refrigerator.

"Oh yes, she's quite a bright woman. When she first got sick, she was in and out of the hospital. She tried having home care four times a day but she didn't like it. Meals On

Wheels brought food but most of it just ended up in the garbage. Truth is, she wanted to be in hospital. She still insisted on driving herself to every appointment. Finally, she got bad enough to be admitted, about a week before you started coming." As Peg finishes speaking, a man comes in the room. It's the same man I saw pacing in the hallway with the chip bag.

"Pastor Mark." Peg stands. *Ah,* I think, *this explains the Daily Bread readings.* Pastor Mark is someone I like immediately. He's in his 40s, has a shaved head and bright blue eyes, and is wearing jeans and a t-shirt. Peg introduces us and we shake hands. Then, he goes right to Ellie's side, picks up her hand and bends to her with ease and gentleness.

"Hey Eleanor," he says softly. "It's good to see you."

Then, he just stands there, his big frame bent over, holding her hand and watching her face with a tender intensity. Something shifts in the room. The space between them is filled with a collected energy, a quality of presence to each other that is sent out and returned. Peg and I lower our eyes like a prayer is being offered. We continue like this for several silent minutes.

Finally, Pastor Mark straightens and there's four of us in the room again. He pulls up a chair and sits. He's got several other people to visit, he says, but begins to tell us a story about going to Ellie and Ralph's place for a barbecue.

"Eleanor was out by the barbecue, turning the meat on low flames, and I asked her if she saw many bears out there. Their trailer is near pretty dense woods," he adds. "She told me, 'Oh yeah, we see lots of them. Usually the dogs go crazy barking. But if I'm outside and one comes by, I've got this.' And from the other side of the barbecue, she picked up one of the largest knives I've ever seen and waved it around." He laughs. "And that," he says, "is Eleanor."

The three of us laugh together and the moment is warm and saturated with affection for this woman around whom we sit. I'm filled up with gratitude for Ellie being spoken of in this way.

Afterwards, when I leave the hospital and walk out into the open air, I think of Ellie living north of town among huge Douglas firs, caring for dogs and scaring away bears. I think of her hospital room and of its total absence of the natural world, where trees and rocks and wind are shuttered out by walls and windows. I think of the floor, where no foot would tread bare, and where washing is done by a waterless lather. I think of the airless room that severs any kinship with the salty ocean and the cedar-scented wind. This is Ellie's dying space.

It's little wonder she feels she is suffocating.

Day 10

It's 6:40 p.m. by the time I arrive to see Ellie. The people of this town love festivals and we spent the day with my brother, sister-in-law and kids at the Canada Day celebrations on the beach. There was live music, bouncy castles and kid games, and a line of vendors selling art and jewelry. We ate pieces of custard-filled cake baked into the shape of a giant maple leaf. We were hot and tired by the time we got home and I quickly ate some leftovers before driving to the hospital.

Except for the intake nurse and a man reading a book in the waiting area, the lobby is empty. The 4th floor is quiet too, with patients already in their rooms awaiting the next shift of nurses due at 7 p.m. The near-silence is a contrast to the noisy celebrations of a short time ago.

In Ellie's room, someone has cleaned up the side table, taking away the eight boxes of renal shake that had accumulated. The tube of oxygen running from the wall into Ellie's nose now passes through a plastic container of water in an effort to hydrate it and reduce Ellie's sense of dryness. On the white board someone has drawn mountains, a few wiggly lines of water and a big sun with the words, *Happy Canada Day!* When I move the chair next to Ellie's bed, it squeaks and Ellie wakes up.

"Hi Anna." She offers me her hand, which I readily take as her eyes close again. Her fingers are white next to my tanned ones. It occurs to me how differently our two bodies are experiencing this summer. In February, I had been weaned off another chemotherapy and in these last few months, had felt stronger and more energetic. Acutely aware of this, I had taken advantage of hiking and swimming as much as I could. I remember the summers I couldn't swim, central lines threaded into veins near my heart then plunging out of my body into open air through a slit in my skin. At times, those two cords for chemo hung like chains from my chest, both protecting and restraining my life.

Six summers earlier in Ontario, the young soya beans popped up in green rows from the dark-soiled field behind our house as I prepared for my first transplant. Since so much of my healing came from being in or near nature, living inside of an isolation room for two-and-a-half weeks at the beginning of summer was something I worried about.

The room I was given had one small window, unfortunately positioned behind the bed so that I could not see out of it. I had taken pictures of the soya shoots, the pear blossoms and the morning sky, of the ways that creation was breaking itself open for life's sake. These were avatars for what I hoped would happen in me. I needed the ground of my body to be broken open by a rush of fresh life. I kept the pictures on my computer, thinking that they would be a comfort while in the hospital. But in the end, to cope, I simply stopped thinking about being outside. It was just too difficult. Now, this summer holds renewed hope for a lasting remission. For Ellie though, each passing day means increasing doses of drugs with decreasing amounts of energy. This summer will be Ellie's last.

I concentrate on Ellie's arm, paying attention to its details. Ellie's skin changes on a day-to-day basis with the amount of fluid her body retains. Today, her fingers are formed into knuckle-less puffs, the wrinkles of her hand pushed smooth and taut. Her arm is swollen, the dark pigment of her liver spots stretched to a slightly bigger size. The thin sheath of skin that holds the fluid inside is itself parched, drying and cracking.

This arm is dying, I think. *This arm is alive.* I look at my own arm, the bones of my wrist and elbow. *This arm is alive. This arm is dying.* Our arms joined, I recognize the reality that neither of us knows exactly where, in the entirety of our lives, that we stand.

When I was younger, I imagined my life as a long horizontal line, stretching from my birth at year zero to somewhere around 80 years. Certainly not less than 70. I based my decisions and efforts around the amount of time I unconsciously calculated that remained. The truth is that my life, like most, has never been a straight stroke. None of us know exactly where we are on our own lifeline. We have a date for its beginning but little insight into when it will end.

When have we passed the midline, the apex, from living to dying? Is there an apex? In truth, I am no more alive than Ellie is in this moment. We are always living, always dying.

I slip my feet out of my shoes and am startled by the socks I'm wearing, a gag-gift from my sister. They are purple, with green leaves and ivy. The side of each one reads, *Your ass is grass.* I laugh and fold my feet under me.

Someday, sister. Someday.

12

Hallelujah:
Praise, joy, thanks;
A yell of glee;
Whoo hoo!

Years 2 & 3

I had been admitted to the hospital for the transplant in mid-June. Everything went as planned. I shaved my head (the third time). My immune system dropped to undetectable levels. For a week, I felt so exhausted that I did not leave the bed except for the bathroom. As the chemo damaged my digestive system, I got terrible diarrhea, though I hardly ate at all. I was weighed every morning, not to monitor the expected weight loss but to make sure I wasn't gaining water weight, a sign that my kidneys had stopped functioning. I didn't read or watch movies or listen to music. I don't even remember speaking much. I laid in the silence of this sterile place, listening to the lavish drum of my heartbeat.

And then, right on the doctor's predicted schedule, my blood counts began to recover. I started to feel better. I began to eat, then sit up, then walk again. By the time I left the hospital, what I craved most was freshness. Fresh air, fresh vegetables, fresh bedsheets.

A fresh life.

* * *

August, two months later. The summer had been shared by a complementary sense of both numbness and sharpness. It was still too difficult to really process what I had come through and too early to know if it had even worked. I spent hours on the swing in the yard, looking up and watching the summer breeze move against the leaves on the trees. My body and my thinking mind rested but parts of my awareness seemed heightened, clearer than ever. The sun, the heat, food, breath, laughter — were continuous gifts to the senses. The freshness I had so deeply craved came to me through simply being alive. I was grateful, everyday.

* * *

A follow-up scan and then a week before the results are due. But two days later, the phone rings and it's Colleen, the nurse practitioner calling.

"Listen, I just got your results back and I couldn't wait until you came in. The scan is *clear*, Anna. The transplant worked. You're cancer-free." Worked. Clear. Free.

Making plans for the future, *for a future*, is a luxury and one that I had reluctantly surrendered. I had been trained to make plans. I worked hard in school so I could attend more school so I would get a job in order to make money and save money and so retire and begin living. I was very good at planning. Then arrived the moment when living many more moments seemed unlikely. I saw that I had not fully inhabited many of the moments I had already been given. Planning is important but it is based on an assumption that most of us share — that there will be a future to plan for.

In the months after the scan results, I entered an exceptional time, a time that lasted almost two years. I began to explore and live into my own rhythm of being. Each day became like a droplet of water, formed from the condensation of my past, held in the present moment, and ready to pour out into my future. Enfolded together, these formed the immediate orb of my life, full and nourishing.

I began looking for my own apartment, finding one I liked in a 1920s building in downtown Windsor. My unit was a tiny one, squished in the middle of the building. It had walls that rounded to the ceilings and built-in bookcases. The kitchen sink was slightly off-centre and the taps in the bathroom turned the wrong way. The old windows looked to the skyline of Windsor and Detroit and the wind rattled their decaying frames into a fine layer of dust that constantly covered the furniture. I watched the GM Tower turn from blue to red to blue again. Sometimes cats scrapped in the alleyway and there were sirens most nights because of the humans scrapping at the bars a few blocks away. It was 350-square-feet of pure bliss.

Six months after the scan, I decided to return to work part-time. I enjoyed teaching and missed my students and coworkers. I also finally had enough energy to dedicate to work. At the first staff meeting I attended after my return, a coworker turned to me and said aloud, "I can't believe you're actually sitting here." Everyone cheered. What he meant was, *Wow, it really did not look good for you last year. We all thought that was it. But here you are — not dead!*

In the evenings, I walked. My apartment was on one of the oldest boulevards in the city, lined with Victorian homes and aged trees — white oaks, black walnut, magnolia and honey locust. I walked under their shelter, more often looking up than ahead. I walked along the edge of the Detroit River, towards the Ambassador Bridge. Or, I went to Jackson Park, to its gardens and rectangular pools of water. I took note of the progression of flowers; pansies to tulips to geraniums to mums. I sometimes stopped to pick a weed or two and to smell the cedar hedge before turning back towards home. These walks were times of transition and taking stock, of loosening the day, of paying attention, of settling and of joy at all that my life had become.

Once while returning from a walk, I was thinking about the people I most admired, all who were from various backgrounds and careers and living very different lives. What was it, precisely, that I admired so much? I realized then that the unifying thread was what I hungered for most: they were living their lives *exactly how they wanted*. It wasn't a self-obsessed, achieving kind of life, but a living in which their authenticity automatically included the wellbeing of others.

As I returned thinking these thoughts, I put the key in the lock of the wooden front door and turned it. Simultaneously, something in me unlocked too, and before the realization had fully formed, I was on the steps with my head in my hands.

I had fashioned my life on many *shoulds* and fears and must-dos. I had unconsciously lived this life while imagining and idealizing a preferable one. But the cancer key, the

suffering key — the almost-dying key — had unlocked my
hungry life. What I admired wasn't a critically-acclaimed
way of being, but an authentic one. It was simple and profound and *in me all along.*

There on those steps, head in hands, fresh from *w-
awe-king,* I realized that I was finally someone I admired.

* * *

A year after the stem cell transplant, I threw a re-
birth-day party in the backyard. The giant slab cake was for
a one-year-old, a rubber ducky theme. We wore party hats.
My best friend gave me a bracelet with a charm on it; one
side was engraved with my original birthday date, the other
with my transplant date. The doctors told me that because
my immune system had been destroyed and replaced, it was
again like that of a one-year-old. I would need to be re-im-
munized with childhood vaccinations. I figured I would now
get an extra 34 years of life since I was considered a baby
again.

Out in the yard, a group of friends played music
and sang. The three of them once came to the hospital when
I was there for one of my extended stays. We planned a party in the atrium, the glassed-in room with plants, a fish tank
and a rooftop balcony that had been a haven for me. I was
late for the party, having waited for a nurse to flush my
chemo line. Fifteen people were already there, crowded
around veggie trays and drinks. We ordered pizza, delivered
up the elevators to the 4th floor. We talked and laughed and
sang together. The trio finished the afternoon with Leonard
Cohen's *Hallelujah.* We cried, looking at each other with feelings of love and gratitude for the deep friendship we shared.

Now, sitting out on the lawn, they played it again. *Love is not a victory march. It's a cold and it's a broken Hallelujah.*

One full year cancer-free. It felt like victory, though hard-won. Statistics told me that relapse was most likely to happen in the first two years post-transplant. If I made it to two years, the odds of having a sustained remission greatly increased. I was halfway there.

A few weeks after the party, I finished teaching and flew to Europe for six weeks of travelling with my best friend, Sophie. We went to Belgium, the Netherlands, England, Ireland, France, Italy and Spain. It was there one day, while sitting in a courtyard having a cold drink after exploring the city that I turned to her and said, "You know, yesterday was the first day in two years that I didn't think about having cancer." Hallelujah.

I flew home in August, tired but happy. I had been healthy enough to travel — to fly with hundreds of people and their different germs, to walk new streets for hours without unwarranted tiredness, to be out of arms-reach of blood work and fixed appointments. I returned to my apartment, to teaching, and to my beloved rhythm of life.

13

Kairos:
A time when the right conditions appear;
A time for crucial action;
The supreme moment.

Eleanor

Day 11

After a warm and windy day, a light rain has begun to fall. It's been an unseasonably wet start to summer. Walking across the parking lot, I see Pastor Mark coming from the opposite direction towards the entrance. We meet at the doors.

"Hi Anna," he says. He's remembered my name.

"Going to see our lady?" I ask.

"Yes, and a few others."

This normally quiet hospital becomes almost deserted on weekends. The elevators open immediately to us. We talk about the weekend, the repairs he's making on his truck. When we get to the 4th floor, Pastor Mark says that he's going to do his other visits first and will afterwards come to see Ellie.

Ellie is on her side, deeply asleep. The oxygen tube is pulled from her nose and laying on the pillow next to her. I look into her face and then bring one arm around to her back. I begin to rub her back in long, slow movements. She is warm and stays asleep. Up and down, up and down. After a few minutes, she shifts and briefly opens her eyes.

"Hi Ellie, it's Anna. Do you want your oxygen in?" She does and so I place the two soft prongs back in her nose and thread the tube around her earlobes. After watching it done by the nurses a few times, I now get it right. She sleeps again. The blanket has fallen from her arms and I see that her skin is even drier and has begun to flake. There are also faint red marks on her forearms and I wonder if she's been scratching in her sleep.

On the nightstand is a plastic basket full of small bottles. There's a waterless body cleanser, shampoo, conditioner, denture fluid, mouth sponges and mouth rinse. I pull one that's labelled *Body Lotion*. It's unscented, hypoallergenic, paediatric-tested and dermatologist-approved. I dispense some into my hands to warm it, then begin on Ellie's left arm, rubbing the cream into the skin near her shoulder, then moving down towards her elbow, forearm, wrist and hand. I massage between her fingers, which are puffy and cool. I move to her right arm.

The lotion doesn't seem to provide much immediate moisture to her skin, but when Ellie opens her eyes again I ask, "Does that feel good or bad?"

"Good," she answers, relaxing again. I continue. Up and down, up and down. The room becomes a warm muffled cocoon where the only sounds are the low hum of the oxygen machine, the rain falling on the windows, and our breath. Time shifts here, in all directions and dimensions.

The ancient Greeks had two words to describe the form and essence of time. *Chronos* is the quantitative, orderly passing of seconds, minutes, hours and days. *Chronos* gives us a tool against which we can concretely measure, record and grapple with, the stages of our life's unfolding.

The second aspect of time, *Kairos,* can be translated as *the supreme moment. Kairos* moments are qualitative ones, ripe with opportunity and a sense of ease, abundance and rightness. *Kairos* can be likened to the brief moment that opens between the arrow's release and its target, or to the fabric's gap before the thread tugs over it. It is a moment weighted with intention, precision and gathered energy. In the *kairos* moment, the archer and weaver, arrow and thread, target and cloth become unified.

We create *chronos,* longing to root ourselves in a specific space and time. But total adherence to *chronos* reduces our life to a tick on the long line of moving history. It ties our sense of self to the body, thoughts and feelings of a particular moment. But *kairos* is not length; it is depth. It does not arrive in your body but in your being. It is ever-present, permanent time. *Chronos does. Kairos is.*

In hospitals, time becomes more meaningful, and less. In many rooms, memories of the past crowd round, competing with apparitions of optimistic futures. Time accelerates, crawls, stands still. With Ellie, *chronos* gives itself over to *kairos.* Time slows, lengthens, intensifies, relaxes. *Kairos* reveals things only seen with the unhurried self — an eyelash flutter, a twitch, a passing look. There is a timelessness for the nearly dead and the nearly born, a moment that gathers unto itself, poised and awaiting what it knows will emerge. Ellie and I enter this time-suspended time, swaddled by the rhythm of our own communication. Up and down, up and down. Warm skin on cool skin. Slow and gentle. Over and over.

When I finish, I pick up the lip moisturizer and apply some to her lips, which have begun to crack. As I recap the lid, Ellie wakes, Pastor Mark walks in and *chronos* resumes.

"Wow Ellie, you're really getting the treatment!" Pastor Mark says, greeting her.

"She deserves it!" I say.

In the small bathroom, I wash the unscented, hypoallergenic, paediatric-tested and dermatologist-approved lotion from my hands then dry them with a rough paper towel. The bathroom is ringed with hand rails and has a shower, toilet, walker, commode, bedpan, call button and more bottles of body care items. When I come out, Pastor Mark is holding Ellie's hand, looking like he will stay awhile. I excuse myself and tell him that I'll be back tomorrow. He doesn't invite me to stay, so I get my bag, bend close to Ellie, and tell her that I'll be thinking of her.

Day 12

"Hurry up! Hurry up!" I think Ellie is talking in her sleep but she opens her eyes. "Hurry up, hurry up! I'm thirsty. Oh my God, I'm so thirsty!" There are three iced drinks on the tray when I come in today. Someone must have refreshed them. Maybe Peg? I hold the renal drink for her and she sucks it fast, then lets out a series of belches and immediately falls back asleep. Thirty minutes later, her eyes fly wide.

"Water! I need water!" She says this with such urgency that I jump up from where I'm sitting beside her. She takes a big gulp of water and coughs.

"Why have I done something wrong? Why did I do that?" she asks.

"Ellie, it's okay. You haven't done anything wrong. You're doing fine." I ask her if she would like lotion on her arms today. She says no. She's agitated, pulling at her sheet and gown. I see the large flap of her disposable brief straining around her hips and folded down under the rolls of her stomach. I wonder how difficult it is to change this brief on someone who is nearly immobile. How long does it take to clean between the folds of skin? How many times a day is this done? Is it enough? Does Ellie have a rash? Does she have bed sores?

In university, I took a double major in psychology and gerontology. During one of the gerontology courses, my professor showed a video on elder abuse. In it was footage of an elderly woman who had been left for long periods in bed without being repositioned. The constant pressure on her back had caused an opening in her skin that had, without care, become infected. The wound became so deep that when the camera lens zoomed in, the bones of her spinal column were visible.

I smooth Ellie's gown, pull the sheet up and fluff her pillow. She raises her hand to me and I clasp it between both of mine, saying, "Gotcha Ellie. I've got you."

I start to say the *Our Father* aloud, a prayer familiar to her.

"What?" she asks.

"I was just going to pray for you Ellie. The *Our Father*."

"Oh, okay." She closes her eyes and I pray her asleep, my voice becoming quieter with each repetition. I marvel again at the paradox of this woman asleep in the bed, of whom I know so little and know so intimately. I gently place her hand down and tuck the blankets close around her. As I move from the bed, Ellie wakens, agitated again and asking, "Where are you going?"

I bend to her. "Would you like me to stay?"

"Oh, yes."

"Of course, Ellie. I will be here with you. And when you fall asleep, I'll go and will come back tomorrow. Okay?"

"Okay."

I hesitate to leave, a little more so today. Why she is asking me to stay? Is she afraid? How will she be when she wakes up? Is this the last time I will see her? I sit with the aloneness of Ellie's dying. The idea of Ellie, anxious and dying, seems unacceptable to me. Yet I am helpless to fully solve this aloneness. I try breathing calmness for both of us. *Inhale* — calm presence when Ellie wakes up. *Exhale* — calm trust that Ellie is helped and held by forces greater than me.

After a few minutes, I walk towards the elevator. I see Pastor Mark at the end of the hall, beginning his visits. I smile.

Day 13

Ellie's lying straight in bed, her hands folded over her chest. I wonder if she's *taken a turn*, as my mother would say. But as I sit down, she wakes up.

"How long have you been here?"

"Just arrived," I say. She takes the pink sponge stick I offer and moves it around inside of her mouth, teeth-less today. The stick has white gummy bits on it when she hands it back to me to throw out.

"What's wrong with me?" she asks. I notice a thin brown line through her right blue iris.

"I think it's your kidneys, Ellie. Are you worried?"

"Yes," she says, but when I ask her more about it, she closes her eyes.

I do small tasks. I run a clean washcloth under cool water then over her forehead, cheeks, neck, arms and hands. I apply lotion to her skin. I take her water jug and cup to the lounge to fill. There is a man in jeans and a checkered shirt sitting at a table, pulling at a box of tissues. He reminds me of my dad, whose restless nature would be tested by *chronos* in this place.

Ellie sleeps most of the hour. At times, to watch Ellie sleep is to watch her enter another world. Time works in different ways inside of her, too. There are characters and conversations happening at a depth that I can only witness from a distant rim. Once, she opened her eyes and began speaking rapidly in another language.

"Ellie? Ellie, what is it?" I asked, but it was as if she hadn't heard me. I realized then that she was someplace else, speaking to another person in another time. I was looking through a one-way mirror into the room of their conversation; I saw them, but they did not see me.

At other times, Ellie whimpers with increasing intensity. "Don't do that! Don't do that!" she once cried out. I sat terrified at what I may hear next, but she only said, "You want me to eat cookies? That is so funny! That is so funny! Wait. Who are you?"

Ellie's body too, participates in this inner dialogue; moaning, flailing a hand, or moving her face into different expressions. Most pronounced are her groans, coming from deep inside of her. I think of our bodies, open-air containers where the cosmos meets the cell. With each in-breath, the universe fills and feeds us. Particles that have always been and will always be, nestle into us, joining us to the beginning of time and to its end. As Ellie's stomach flattens and her lungs collapse, as her body pushes the universe back out past her vocal cords and into the sky, her body releases its cry. These wails and whimpers seem to be sounds of mutual mourning between Ellie and the universe, as their relationship in this particular form nears its end.

Once more before I leave, Ellie awakens. She looks at me with dampened eyes and says, "I'm still alive?"

It is one part question; the other, lament.

Day 14

Andrew and I arrive early at my brother and sister-in-law's to spend the day with the kids. By mid-afternoon, we're back home where I change my clothes for a work meeting. Afterwards, we need to eat and get to my niece's choir concert where she is performing until 10 p.m. I'm so tired after my meeting that I crawl into bed and nap while Andrew makes dinner. Today is the first day that I do not visit Ellie since meeting her.

On most days I plan to visit Ellie, my mind resists, coming up with ways to convince me that visiting is a chore or that there are more preferable things to do. My habit energy tells me to keep busy, to skip a visit or shorten it in order to get other things done. In the beginning, I was tempted to listen, especially when this voice mixed with my general anxiety about sitting with someone who is dying.

But as I continued my centring practice, I began to recognize this voice as the part of my ego that is uncomfortable in situations where I am not in control or do not feel competent. Once I named this anxiety as such, it largely lost its persuasion, though it periodically continued to try. When sitting with Ellie I am often filled with a quiet stillness, devoid of anxious thoughts and agitated movement. In this state I hear something else: *There is little more important than this. There is nowhere that I'd rather be.* Today, missing our visit for the first time, I know this to be true.

I realize that these daily visits are not required, but this isn't about filling volunteer hours. I *want* to see Ellie. Ellie is actually dying and I don't want her to do it alone.

Day 15

After a restless night's sleep, I've spent another full day with the kids. By the end of the afternoon, I feel tired and short-tempered. I decide to go see Ellie while I still have the energy. In fact, today I feel an urgency to visit. Being with Ellie has become a refuge of sorts, a space beyond expectation, achievement and activity. When I push the door open to the semidarkness and quiet, everything but our two breathing bodies falls away.

There is a power imbalance inherent between volunteers and the people they serve. In my relationship with Ellie, my bodily strength and her bodily weakness creates a gap in power between us, increasing her vulnerability to me. The possibility exists of my having some advantage or authority over her. I must be careful of power's subtle nature, of misplaced good intentions. I feel this way about naming Ellie's space as a personal refuge, of using her dying as a place of peace for me. I only mean to say that there is a quality of being that surrounds Ellie which, however unintended, blesses me in return.

The more I am with Ellie — the more carefully that I can watch and listen, or close my eyes and breathe with her — the more sensitized I become to the underlying landscape we inhabit. It longs to emerge and waits patiently for my attentiveness. In the moments I awaken, in the moments when I allow myself to be receptive and responsive, the stark sterility of the hospital room becomes a gift whose purpose is served by simply fading away. These white walls become a blank canvas that sacrifices itself in order to give rise to the living tableau that is unfolding within it.

Dying arises in front of me with nuanced clarity. I watch the energies of life and death at work in Ellie. They move together, one asserting while the other recedes; constantly reorganizing themselves into new dimensions. Ellie dances with life; death cuts in. Her nails keep growing but her digestion slows. She talks in bursts then sleeps long spells. She is thirsty though she cannot eat. The absolute dependency between life and death, the ultimate of mysteries, stretches out before me.

If I can sustain my attention and patience long enough in these moments, the physical processes of Ellie's body also begin to ebb. The externals of Ellie's life — independence, work, appearance, movement — begin to pass away. This is the great, difficult and necessary act that dying requires of us. Here, death claims its rightful jurisdiction.

Yet, as death begins its external clear-cutting, it can also fuel an inverse expansion. Energy is gathered unto itself as generative inner growth. For as far as the body declines, the inner self swells in strength. This is the Self beyond wounds, illness and loss, beyond striving, achievement and the need for praise. It is the Self untouched by the transient, the superficial or the brief, however positive or negative we judge these to be. It is the Self that finds its identity in a larger Presence. Though death takes its place within us, so too does death bow to this primary and rightful authority of the human being's spirit. The body's infirmity not only sanctions the primacy of this spirit, but often gives birth to it.

It is a training to see beyond the immediacy of the body to the depths of being. In awe, I watch this masterpiece unfurl in Ellie, stoked by the power of her dying. Beyond holding this awe, my role here is simply to allow the energy of her dying to change me.

The art of Ellie's death is both unsettling and enriching. The dynamic processes happening in Ellie happen in every living being that ever comes to this earth. They will happen in me. Ellie's death is my death, is our death. And so, the balance of perceived authority shifts. Ellie surrenders to her masterpiece and in doing so, takes on the part of teacher.

Death asks me to see in Ellie the likeness of my own fragility. Death gives me the chance to examine my misplaced trust in passing commodities; the obsessions, assumptions and performances that impersonate my life. If I am wise, I will learn from Death now, rather than waiting for a day when Death may not be so patient with me. If I am wise, I will learn not only from Death, but from illness, failure, divorce, and loss, teachers versed in sifting the short-lived from the lasting.

And if I am wise, I will let Death point me to its own Master — Love — and to Love's accomplices; Joy and Beauty. And if I learn, I will take the brushes handed to me by these teachers — brushes dripping with meaning — and I will use them to colour the contours of my own beautiful, vulnerable life.

14

Rend:
To split apart by violence;
To tear the hair or clothing as a sign of anger, grief or despair;
To lacerate mentally or emotionally.

Dad

In the three years following his diagnosis and treatment, Dad enjoyed retirement. My sisters taught him to use a desktop computer and the internet. His typing was slow but determined. Soon, he was trading chain letter jokes with his retired friends and looking up recipes for *Slow Cooker Chicken, New Orleans Gumbo* and *Classic Chili Con Carne.* And in those years, Dad had kept his promise and had walked me down the aisle on my wedding day.

Then, when everything had seemed to stabilize in our lives again, Dad began coughing. Spittle and phlegm flew from his stoma into his handkerchief. We waited, hoping it was a cold or the flu; something that would pass. It continued.

More tests. This time, the cancer was found in Dad's lungs. Dad was referred to Toronto General Hospital for surgery to remove the tumours, a surgery the doctors deemed successful.

Mom and Dad's 30th wedding anniversary fell a few months later and the six of us planned a surprise dinner at their favourite Italian restaurant. A few years before, Dad had crafted two large stained-glass windows for the restaurant's owner. The night of the party, our friends and extended family sat under the glass that had been cut and set into thick vines and bursting grapes, telling stories of Dad and Mom's life together. We raised our glasses of wine to honour the life they had made, the life that had created the six of us, and the life that had so positively influenced the lives of those in the room.

I was 26 years old. That night, the wine and the bread, the stained glass and stained mouths, the toasting of life and the dying body, the sacrifice and the intimacy and the love — more than anything, the love — brought me the closest I've been to the altar of communion.

* * *

Spring arrived. Mom and Dad planned a long-awaited road trip to the west coast for July. We hoped the warmth and sun would help Dad's body and spirits. Over the winter months, he had continued experiencing fatigue and fierce coughing spells.

In late May, we gathered at Mom and Dad's to celebrate my sister's and Mom's birthday. Mom turned 60. Dad barbecued out in the yard, and we had cake and ice cream. A few hours later, I was back at my own place, practicing guitar. Though scratchy and hesitant, I had learned to play the Beatles' *Let It Be.* I called the house to let my brother hear my progress.

Mom answered the phone and spoke in a tone that I had seldom heard, but would come to recognize. It was the voice under her words that caught me, a voice that said, *I am terrified. Things are out of control. Help.*

Dad was in a coughing fit so badly that he couldn't catch his breath. An ambulance had been called but they were alone, everyone having gone out after dinner. I lived close to the hospital and left immediately to meet the ambulance when it arrived while Mom followed the ambulance in the car.

Twenty minutes later I was pacing back and forth in front of the *Emergency Personnel* doors. I knew Dad was back there; he wasn't in the waiting room. Finally, a paramedic burst through the swinging doors. It was Crista. A friend. Crista and I volunteered together. She was also a paramedic in our town and happened to be on duty. She swept me into a huge hug.

"He's okay," she said. She led me through the doors to where Dad was already lying in a bed.

"Dad!" I bent to kiss him, grabbing his hands. "Mom's on her way. She'll be here any minute." He wasn't coughing, but was quiet; anxiety lined his face. Crista left us to attend to her next call. I pulled up a chair and sat next to Dad, my hand on his arm, not knowing what to say. We waited.

Then, Dad was caught and pulled under by a force more powerful than either of us. The fit came with fury. With each cough, Dad's eyes bulged from his head, both from the sheer physical force of his convulsing lungs and from the fear that gripped him. I stood there, absolutely helpless except to watch this terror take hold in my father. Finally, he ejected phlegm directly from his stoma into his handkerchief. Released from its grip, he lay back exhausted. I bit my lip and tried not to cry.

Mom arrived. Dad was put on oxygen, admitted to the hospital for a few days, and scheduled for more tests.

> *And when the night is cloudy*
> *There is still a light that shines on me*
> *Shine until tomorrow*
> *Let it be*

* * *

We all took turns visiting Dad while the tests were done. One evening, after visiting Dad in the afternoon, I went home to prepare dinner. My sister called. *Could you come back up?* The whole family was there with Dad. I told her that I was just cleaning up and would be there soon. Fifteen minutes later, my brother phoned. *What are you doing? Can you come?* I dropped the dishcloth and drove to the hospital.

Dad was born in 1934 in Queens, New York to a large Irish Catholic family. During his upbringing, the men in Dad's life comfortably expressed joviality and anger, but feelings like tenderness and sadness were reserved from public display. Through much of Dad's life, his own way of relating seemed much the same. During my teenage and young-adult years though, Dad had become softer, more easily moved to emotion, and quicker to hug and kiss. As I matured too, we shared more time together and developed a deeper relationship.

Now entering that hospital room, my father's face was a patchwork of pain, fear and sadness. I had rarely seen these manifest on any face I had known during my innocent life. I knew Dad had suffered during his life because there were times and topics he refused to talk about. I had just never *seen* his suffering before and seeing suffering on a face you love penetrates you differently than merely knowing about suffering. Mom, my two sisters and two brothers flanked Dad on both sides of the bed railings and I saw this suffering as it distributed itself in varying forms across the faces of my most beloved: Heartache, agony, anger, despair.

I never sang *Let It Be* again.

* * *

The doctor told us that Dad had four months to live. The cancer had returned to his lungs and metastasized. It was deemed untreatable except for palliative comfort care. Mom made arrangements for Dad to come home, setting up regular nursing care and getting details for a hospital bed to be delivered. We purchased a soft, padded recliner and positioned it in front of the large window in the living room where Dad could be among us and watch the spring turn into summer. Father's Day was two weeks away and our older brother planned to bring his family then in order to spend time with Dad.

But Dad got worse, fast. He began sleeping more. He stopped eating and his pain kept increasing, preventing him from being discharged. We had a family friend, Debbie, who nursed on the oncology unit. One afternoon, she asked my mom, my siblings and me to join her in the *Family Room*.

"I know the doctor said Mike has about four months left." She took a deep breath. We held ours.

"I'm sorry, but I've worked here a long time. I've seen how this goes. It won't be months. It will be weeks." She described how Dad could die during a coughing fit, and that

Mom needed to decide on resuscitation orders and end-of-life care.

My eyes met the eyes of my sisters and brothers, our young hearts torn open so violently that the pain gushed into our bodies, up-welled and overflowed from the outlet of our eyes. It was simply too much to be held inside. But no matter how much or how often we seemed to drain ourselves, this river was too powerful, too full and too raging to be exhausted. I could not look at my mother.

That night, I crawled into bed and read the glossy pamphlets I had taken from the hospital about the changes we could expect as Dad's body died. *Decreased desire to eat. Blood pooling under the skin. Loss of bladder control.* I sobbed. I felt utterly traumatized. *Lacerated and split apart by violence.*

And there was nothing to be done but to be split open by this pain and to let it do its holy work. And it was his cancer, not mine, that became the catalyst for my life's radical change. His death would change it all.

15

Sign:
A gesture by which a thought is expressed;
Something indicating the presence or existence of something else;
A posted command, warning, or direction.

Eleanor

Day 16

The head of the bed is positioned upright, but Ellie is slumped to one side, her head resting between the pillows and the bedrail. I tell her quietly that I will help move her onto the pillows, which I gently do. Ellie remains asleep. Today, I sit and watch her face.

Her breathing is irregular, her lungs going long seconds without an inhale, then pulling in a series of quick, shallow breaths. I try to match this pattern. Starving my lungs of oxygen and then flooding them rapidly is both uncomfortable and difficult to sustain.

I begin to breath slow, easy breaths. Soon, I notice a pattern. I breathe in, *1-2-3-4-5-6*. Ellie's body is still. She does not inhale. I breathe out, *6-5-4-3-2-1*. Ellie's lungs take in two fast breaths. She moans as she does this, her body trying to replenish its life force. When she stops breathing for so long, she looks as though she has died and each time, I wonder if she has.

The afternoon that my dad died, his breathing was like this. My mom, sister and I were with him in a palliative care room, one of four down a small hospital wing. Across the hall, another woman sat alone with her dying father. One day, the woman came to the door and asked if I would watch her father for a few minutes while she went to the cafeteria for coffee. I stood in the doorway where I could see both fathers. It was from this doorway that I watched these men begin to die away from their loved ones.

Within a few short minutes, Dad's breathing noticeably changed, his inhales becoming farther apart and raspy sounding. I said aloud, "It's happening." I left the doorway for Dad's side, abandoning the woman's father for my own. Between Dad's breaths, my mom, sister and I looked to one another, searching for confirmation that our lives had just changed. The time between Dad's breaths seemed impossibly long until finally, it was impossibly long. Just minutes later, the man in the next room died, too. His daughter returned with her coffee. I heard her wails.

Inhale. Exhale. Soon, Ellie and I are in a rhythm, my breath the steady low beat beneath her sharper one. I close my eyes and we are in deep rest together. Time lengthens between Ellie's breaths.

1-2-3-4-5-6-7-8. Awhile later, *1-2-3-4-5-6-7-8-9-10-11-12.*

Ellie doesn't wake for water or for anything else today. After awhile, I hear the door push open. I expect Pastor Mark, who often visits at the end of his workday. Instead, a tiny woman stands with her hand on the door. She has shoulder-length grey hair and thick slip-proof socks on her feet. She is so small that the strings of her gown are wrapped twice around her waist. She takes a few tentative steps in and looks around Ellie's room with uncertainty. I immediately see that she does not know where she is.

"Hi there" I say. "How can I help you?"

"I'm looking for a bit of water." Her voice is so soft that I almost miss her English accent.

"Ah yes. You're looking for the lounge. Let me show you." In the hall, I slow my step so I can walk beside her. I ask her what room is hers.

"Fifteen, I think. Or sixteen." These are the rooms next to Ellie's. "We've got a bit to walk," I say.

In the lounge, I pour her some water and hand it to her. She is grateful.

"And so I'll stay here?" she says. It is a question, and one she is looking for me to answer.

"Yes, you can stay here. There's a couch," I gesture, "and a TV and some magazines." But she walks to the window, looking out to the towering pines moving in the rain. I leave her there, looking into the sky.

I now stand next to Ellie. How many breaths does she have left? It seems strange that there will be a day when I won't see her again. On any meaningful level, envisioning the world without someone who is currently living is almost an impossibility for me. I smooth Ellie's hair though it has hardly moved. I run my hand across her forehead and cheek. Her skin is warm and pink today.

The tiny woman is walking by again, holding the arm of a woman wearing a red tracksuit. The woman asks, "And where is your room?"

"This one I think, and the first bed?" They've turned into a doorway and I hear the woman in red promise to bring a cup of tea.

I gather my raincoat and bag and bend close to Ellie, whispering, "Thank you, Ellie. Thank you. God love you. Sleep well and I'll see you tomorrow."

I'm almost at the elevators when the woman in red comes out of the lounge with the promised tea in a mauve plastic cup. She stops to speak to a nurse.

"Yes, she wanders the hall all day, in and out of rooms," I hear the nurse say. This woman, our elder, who walks in circles in the safety of strangers.

Day 17

On the seventeenth day of knowing Ellie, the door is closed when I come down the hall. I pause, then tentatively push it open. I see the women first. One is in her early 20s, sitting next to someone who appears to be her mother.

Ellie's church friends finally came, I think.

Then I see the legs, long and skinny, clothed in blue pyjama pants and propped up by two pillows under the knees. The feet are bare and bony. Still, it takes me what seems a long time. It takes until I see his face. *Gaunt* is the word my mother would use. Synonyms flood my mind. *Hollow. Haggard. Rawboned. Emaciated. Wasted.* The women look at me with expectation.

"I'm so sorry," I say. "I'm in the wrong room." I back out and close the door. *I'm not in the wrong room*, I think. *They are.* This is not Ellie's room, I know. It is a palliative care room and Ellie is just one human being in the stream of human beings who will use this bed to die.

I practically run to nurses' station, my body responding to the rising awareness of what this means, while blocking it from fully accessing my mind. It senses that we are about to hear something we had hoped would come on a more distant day. I speak to a nurse seated at the desk. My words come out as tentative questions.

"I'm looking for Eleanor Davis? She was in 444?" The nurse says *Um*, and starts flipping through papers. Behind the nurse stands a doctor wearing glasses and a stethoscope around his neck.

"She was moved to Woodhaven this morning," he says, looking up from the notes in his hand.

"Really?" I ask. Woodhaven is a long term care facility. Apparently, Ellie's condition was stable for too long. The man who now lays in 444 is closer to death. I nod and thank them, then reverse my steps down the elevator, through the lobby and to my car, aware that my daily visits here are over.

In the car, I realize that I don't actually know where I'm going. There are several care facilities in town and I'm not sure which one is Woodhaven. One street over from the hospital there are several, so I decide to start there. The first has recently opened and has big windows and well-kept gardens. It's trimmed in wood and the entrance is tucked under a peaked foyer. I slow in front of the building, hoping it's this one. The sign reads *Douglas Suites*.

I circle onto the road again and pull up to the next one. It's an older building, about a third of the size with grey-green siding. There's a small placard on the front that reads: *Woodhaven Extended Care*. I park the car.

The entrance has a waist-height gate that looks like a baby gate. It is locked. Next to it is a sign that reads,

WOODHAVEN EXTENDED CARE

PRESS 1234 TO ENTER

PLEASE ENSURE THE GATE IS
CLOSED BEHIND YOU

I punch the code into the number pad and the gate releases. I close it behind me until the lock clicks. Next, there are two pairs of automated doors. Between them is a hand sanitizer pump and another sign:

PLEASE ENSURE
NO RESIDENTS
FOLLOW YOU OUTSIDE

The second set of doors open into a huge room that looks like a lodge. There's easily sixty old folk in the room. Some sit in cushioned chairs, canes hooked on tables while they play cards or checkers and drink coffee. Others sit looking through the windows at the bird feeders hung outside, cups of tea in front of them. A corner of the room holds a TV showing *Jeopardy!*. There are also spots at the tables where chairs have been pulled away and wheelchairs rolled up. Some of these people are asleep, hunched forward in their chairs or heads back, mouths open. A few of the wheelchairs are completely tilted back, the person in them perpetually observing the ceiling. For so many people in one room, it's surprisingly quiet.

As I walk through the centre of the room towards the nurses' desk at the back, all eyes seem to turn towards me. A scream comes from down the hall, but no one seems concerned. A man calls out, "No Lieutenant!", then relaxes into indiscernible chatter.

117

Hallways radiate like spokes from the nurses' station and I'm pointed down one labelled *Fir Grove*. Along the wall are large-print signs that read *THOMAS'S ROOM*, with arrows pointing all the way to what I assume must be *THOMAS'S ROOM*. The number for Ellie leads me to a four-person room, each bed separated by privacy curtains. Ellie's bed is on the far left, next to a large window that casts natural light into the room. Outside, there's a hedgerow and a bird feeder. Ellie is awake, her oxygen tube now hooked to a portable machine rather than the wall.

"Hi Ellie, it's Anna." My smile must be warm because I am almost giddy to see her.

"Am I ever glad to see you!" Ellie says. I am glad too, but before I can say so, she continues. "They're stingy with the water here. I want a glass of real water."

I bend down close to her. "Ah! No problem Ellie," I say. "I know exactly where to get some." We are conspiring together to beat the system. There is a carafe full of icy water sitting on her tray just behind her line of sight. I make a fuss, swishing the cubes around and then splashing it loudly into a glass. I top it off with a clean straw and pass it to her with a slight bow.

"Here you are, ma'am. Real British Columbian water." She takes a long sip, then leans back heavily on her pillows.

"That is so good."

"How was the move over here?" I ask.

"Not so good." Her mouth downturns as she waves her hand. She pauses and looks around. "Where am I?" she asks.

"Ellie, you moved next door from the hospital, to Woodhaven. You've got a nice new room."

"Oh. I hate rats. I hate…oh, I'm looking for a word. Sab, sab…" she mumbles. *"Saboteur."*

"Is that French, Ellie? Where did you learn that?"

"Yes. French. I was born in Trois Rivières. My parents…" She drifts off.

"I've been there," I tell her. "I drove through on an east coast camping trip. It's beautiful." I sit down, lean my elbows on the bed and take her hand, smiling.

A nurse comes into the room and to Ellie's side, checking her breathing machine. "Is she alright?" she asks.

"Yes, I think so."

"Her call button went off," says the nurse. She looks at me and then down at the bed where Ellie and I are holding hands. "You're leaning on it."

"Oh, I'm so sorry," I say, bringing my hands up quickly.

"No, no, it's okay. I don't want you to stop cuddling." She winks and moves the call button cord up near Ellie's head and walks out.

Ellie opens her eyes again and says, "Know what would taste real good? An ice-cold cola. Mmm." I agree with her, that would taste great. "A cola. Or a root beer. Root beer with ice."

When Ellie falls asleep, I look around at the details of the room. Each resident has a ten-by-ten foot area. Each area has a single bed, nightstand, narrow cupboard and bulletin board. Overhead are mechanized mobility pulleys for lifting people. There is a shared bathroom. Here are signs that this is a permanent home. An heirloom clock hangs on the wall. A quilt is folded at the end of a bed. There are pictures of new babies, graduations and weddings. The white board above Ellie's nightstand reads:

NAME: Eleanor Madeline Davis (Likes to be called Ellie)

D.O.B: April 24th, 1939

DENTURES: Upper   Lower   Own

FOOD: Fluids and fruits. Likes all drinks over ice. CHOKE RISK.

COMMUNICATION: Tires easily when talking.

MOBILITY: 1-person lift; bed alarm; side rails upper and lower. Reposition throughout the day.

A woman in a wheelchair enters the room, pushed by a middle-aged man and followed by three women. They enter the space next to Ellie. The curtain is pulled closed.

"Here we go, Mom," I hear the man say, followed by what sounds like efforts to position the woman into bed. "There! All set! How about another sip of juice?" The voices have a stiff cheeriness. I stand to leave.

At the entrance, the automatic doors don't slide open. I walk a little closer, trying to trigger them with my weight. I look around for a button to press. There isn't one. I wave my arms a little in case there's a motion detector. Nothing. There is no sign, no arrow, no obvious way to leave the building. I stand there, looking around, beginning to feel foolish. The nurses start calling out from the back of the room. They are gesturing for me to turn towards the wall on my right. I do. I don't see anything.

"Look up! Look up!" they shout.

Above me, high enough that I have to reach up, is what looks like a plastic fire alarm cage. Underneath it is a button. I lift the cage and press it. The doors slide open.

PLEASE ENSURE
NO RESIDENTS

FOLLOW YOU OUTSIDE

It's the final thing I see of Eleanor's new home.

16

Devastate:
To reduce to chaos, disorder, or helplessness;
To cause extreme emotional pain;
To destroy much or most of.

Year 4

"How do you feel?" Dr. Marian sat down and wheeled her stool up close to me. I was here to discuss my now-routine CT scan.

"Fine. Great." I said. So great that I had come to the appointment alone. But I knew her, and this, well enough by now. I eyed her. "Why?"

"There is a small spot on your lung. I'm not sure it's cancer. No symptoms?" she asked. I shook my head.

"Your cancer doesn't usually hide itself."

It's true. If my cancer had a personality, it would be the obnoxious and uninvited guest knocking things over in the living room, sending a life's cherished keepsakes to the ground, shattering them. My tumours would invite other tumours over, yelling, *Let's get this thing started!* over their already blaring tune of symptoms. I used to see this as a betrayal, my body shaking with fever and so easily becoming symptomatic. Now, I'm thankful for my body's effort at alerting me that something isn't right. It's this early warning system that has caught the cancer in its early stages.

"Ok," Dr. Marian said. "Let's wait a month then redo the scan. We'll see what it does."

Cue latent paranoia.

I was in the third month of a new relationship. Andrew and I first met in late September, right after my return from Europe. He lived in Toronto, about a four-hour drive away. We slowly increased our conversations until November, when we began spending time together in person. We were so similar that we originally thought we'd be better off as friends. But as time went on, our feelings deepened and we began dating in December. On our first Skype call, I told him about my time with cancer. He listened carefully and then said that it seemed to him that having cancer had led me to a greater depth and authenticity in my life. Meeting Andrew was the final gift in a wondrous year.

But cancer-past and the personal growth it can foster is different than cancer-present. Cancer-present means your partner is bald and sick and that normal dating stops being normal. I was due to meet his family in March, the week of my 35th birthday, right before the follow-up CT scan. Andrew drove with me from Windsor to Toronto and on the four-hour drive, I started a conversation that I had given a lot of thought to.

"You know, if this turns out to be cancer, life is going to get harder. I've been through this before. I will completely understand if a relationship is too much. It's not our fault — we simply haven't had the time to get enough ground between us yet to deal with this. It's truly okay if you decide it's too much." I meant it. I knew that if this was a relapse, the road ahead wouldn't be an easy one. I wouldn't have thought at all badly of him. I also had my own fears and concerns about dealing with a third diagnosis and all that might mean while also doing the work of a new relationship.

When I was finished talking, Andrew reached over, took my hand and said, "I'm fine. Let's keep going. We'll see what comes."

I met his family. We took his grandmother for breakfast, met his parents in High Park, and visited his aunt. On one of our last days there, he took me to the Toronto Zoo. The air was warm with the spring sun and we walked for hours, watching the orangutangs and polar bears and sloths. We were outside of the lionesses cage at the far end of the park when I reached to scratch under my arm. I froze. A lump. My fingers moved over it, making sure. I walked away from the enclosures where Andrew stood and pulled out my phone.

When the nurse answered I explained, "I'm a patient of Dr. Marian. I'm due for a CT scan soon but I just found a lump." She immediately booked me an appointment for the following week. As I pressed the *End Call* button, I turned to see Andrew bending down to right a kicked-over garbage can. I struggled not to cry.

We returned to Windsor to celebrate my 35th birthday with my family. After everyone left, Andrew and Mom took my hands in theirs. As we stood in a circle, they blessed me and prayed for me, telling me that they would be here with me, whatever came. It was the first time that Andrew and Mom met.

* * *

I held in my hands a yellow folder. The Yellow Fold-er. The Yellow Folder for the Newly Diagnosed. It was filled with pages of cancer facts and drug names and support web-sites. I held that yellow folder in my hands, deeply angry. Why yellow? The colour of sunshine and buttercups and my baby niece's hair. It should have been grey for this grey zone I kept plunging into. I had made it 20 out of 24 months to-wards long-term remission.

* * *

The next step, Dr. Marian thought, would be a sec-ond transplant using cells from a donor. Though my bone marrow appeared cancer-free when tested, something about my body's makeup kept producing lymphoma. The process of the previous transplant would be repeated but this time, after the heavy doses of chemo destroyed my immune sys-tem, donor cells (the graft) would be infused into me (the host). The aim was to armour me with an entirely new im-mune system better able to recognize and destroy lymphoma cells.

The risks of this type of transplant are much higher. Transplant-related deaths are primarily due to either graft-versus-host disease (GvHD) or infection. In GvHD, the new-ly-grafted cells perceive the host as foreign and begin to at-tack it. The host doesn't reject the new cells. The new cells reject the host. It is the strength of these new cells that har-bour both a transplant's success and its greatest risks.

Graft-vs-host disease can attack the eyes, skin, respi-ratory tract, gastrointestinal tract, liver and other organs, and can lead to organ failure. There is a terrifying amount of information about GvHD-related death. Even now, while

125

reading about it my body constricts, feeling its violence. While in the hospital for my transplant, I befriended a woman my age who had leukaemia. She was alone much of the time as her husband cared for their two small boys at their home several hours away. She died from severe GvHD a few months after our transplants, the details of which remain too painful to share.

For me, the most hopeful scenario was that one of my siblings would match me on the numerous blood markers needed in order to donate cells. Having a closely-matched related donor lessened the risk of rejection. Each of my siblings had a 25% chance of matching me. If none of them did, my information would be entered into a world-wide database of people searching for an unrelated donor.

So we began. Each of my siblings were sent lab requisitions and each gave blood samples in different parts of North America. The samples were then sent to a specialized lab for analysis. The two closest hospitals that did allogenic or donor transplants were in Hamilton and Toronto. We asked that I be referred to Toronto since Andrew's family, as well as my aunt and uncle, lived there. Before I could be referred, two things needed to happen. We needed to find a donor and the cancer had to shrink, showing that it was still responsive to treatment.

Dr. Marian started me on another round of chemotherapy drugs, one that required hospitalization again. After almost two years away from treatment, my hair had grown in dark curls to my chin. As a teenager, I had begun dying my hair a lighter colour, so I was now seeing my natural hair colour for the first time in about 15 years. I decided I would never colour it again — I was just grateful to have my own hair.

The niece who lived closest to me was now five years old. So that she wouldn't be afraid when I became bald, I asked her dad, my brother-in-law, to shave my head. On a warm spring day, I sat on their back deck and my niece watched as I went bald. *Cool eh?* I said, letting her rub my head. When she later came to visit me in the hospital, I let her play with the buttons on the bed, moving the head and feet up and down in different angles while I said, *Ohh!* and *Ahhh!* and *Watch this!*

During those days back in the hospital, Mom or my sister or a friend would come during the day to keep me company. Andrew came from Toronto and stayed in my apartment. He would come to the hospital in the evenings, sometimes with a veggie pita or something I was craving for dinner, and we would watch a movie on the laptop.

A few weeks into the treatment, Colleen called while I was at home. "Anna, I'm sitting here with the other nurses and we had to call. The donor results just came back. This is incredible, but all six of you have a perfect match in the family. The odds of this are extraordinary." The blood tests showed that my two younger brothers were matches for each other, as were my two younger sisters. My older brother Tom was a match for me.

We were ecstatic. Statistics showed that in cases where a brother donates to a sister, the odds of long-term remission or cure are slightly higher than average, perhaps because of the greater volume of cells that can be collected from men.

Dr. Marian ordered a scan to determine how the treatment was working. Our joy slackened. The scan showed continued cancer growth. Dr. Marian immediate switched the drug regime and we began to wait again. One positive of

my particular cancer was that it was sensitive to chemotherapy and had almost always been reduced by just one
dose. But cancer has the ability to mutate in order to survive,
becoming resistant to treatment over time. We simply had to
wait and see what the cancer would do.

Knowing we had another month to wait, Dr. Marian referred me to the cancer hospital in Toronto with the
hope that by the time the doctors were ready to see me, I
would have a scan that showed the treatment was working. I
asked Dr. Marian what the timeline until transplant would
be. She said, "I don't know. You're not accepted by them
yet." Accepted? I had assumed that if the cancer decreased
and I had a donor, a transplant was inevitable. I didn't know
that I could possibly be denied based on a number of factors. I was scared of the risks of the transplant but I knew
that without it, my disease would eventually progress beyond
what chemotherapy could control. I was booked for an initial intake meeting in Toronto.

17

Prism:

A transparent body used to reflect light;
Two parallel faces;
A medium that distorts, slants or colours what is viewed through it.

Eleanor

Day 18

I stop at the grocery store on the way to see Ellie. I want to bring her a cold drink. I look at the cola bottles. All of them have slogans on their labels: *First Kiss, Best Day, Living the Dream.* I look for one that reads *Death Bed Nostalgia* or *Comfort for a Dying Body.* None are suitable, so I move down and choose a large root beer from the next cooler. After paying, I put it in my backpack and walk up the road to Ellie. When I get to Ellie's room, she's awake and sitting up.

"Good morning," I say, touching her shoulder. "Have you had any breakfast?"

"Hmm. I don't think so," Ellie answers, although it's already 10 a.m. and she has likely received something.

"Guess what I brought?" I ask, leaning down to her so she can see me better. "A root beer. Ice-cold."

Ellie's whole face becomes delight. She reminds me of a child whose entire being lights up with the simplest pleasure.

"How does that sound?"

"More than fantastic."

I get up to fetch a clean cup and ice from the kitchen. On the way out of the room, I hear Ellie say in a voice of wonder, "Roooot beer."

In this dry, pale world, I unscrew the cap. The dark liquid fizzes up and makes a *sheut* sound, waiting to escape into the air. I pour the sugary bubbles over ice and hand it to her. She takes a long drink then lays back, mouth open and eyes wide.

"Oh my God. Thank you, Lord. Thank you." This satisfaction, this pleasure and quenching, is nothing short of holiness.

She has several more sips then lays back, tired again. I take a fresh cloth from her nightstand and run it under cool water. I bring it to her face, where she takes it in her own hands, pressing it to her closed eyes and forehead. For a moment, her face is a shroud.

I think of the ways bodies used to be cared for after death, laid out by loved ones who took it as their duty and right to care for their dead. Multiple hands attending to every crease; a skin-to-skin recollection of that body as a child, parent or lover. The methodical smoothing on of oily spices or careful wrapping in fabric; the tending to a body known to you as intimately as your own and in which you will not see again. I hope that this is what I am offering Ellie; an anointing of her body and spirit not after death, but before.

In this room there are no hymns, only silence. There are no prayer benches, only beds. Hospital gowns become robes as we are ushered into our own inner sanctuary. Root beer serves as wine and our beings, the bread. This space, this physical room, becomes our temple, the altar where we offer our broken bodies in service to the other. It is in this brokenness, *by* this brokenness, that we are brought together. This is as close to the sacred as there is in this world.

Ellie moves the cloth across her face. The shroud is dropped and she opens her eyes. She offers the cloth back to me. She doesn't know that she has cleansed me, too. When our eyes and hands meet she simply says, "Thank you."

Day 19

The sun is hot and bright, finally pulling the temperatures into the high 20s. Friends have arrived from Ontario and we take them to walk a shoreline trail, pointing out the names of nearby islands.

"The air is so fresh and clean here," our friends comment several times. After lunch, I leave them on the front porch to enjoy the afternoon sun with potato chips and cold drinks.

On my way to Ellie's, I pull into a drive-thru and order a small chocolate milkshake. When it's handed to me though the window, I see that it's sponsored by the same cola company. The slogan on the side of the cup reads, *Hangin' Out.* At least that's what Ellie and I will be doing today.

When I arrive at Ellie's room, the curtains are still pulled across the windows and around her bed. I pull them open. Ellie is sleeping, her gown pulled up around her stomach revealing a twisted brief. On the tray table is a dirty cup and a large stainless-steel bowl with something brown stuck to its bottom. The bottle of root beer is still half-full and out of reach. I put the milkshake down and bend to straighten the sheets. The foot of the bed is wet — not like urine but soaking — as if a full glass of liquid was dumped on it.

What the hell? Something in me is deeply pissed-off. I press the red button and a nurse arrives.

"Hi there. I just walked in and the sheets were pulled up around her. The foot of the bed is soaking. Has someone been in here today?" It's clear that I am not pleased. The nurse bends to touch the blankets.

"Oh. How could that have happened?" she says, feeling the degree of wetness. She clears the table and goes for gloves and new sheets. When she returns, she touches Ellie's shoulder to gently wake her. Ellie opens her eyes.

"Eleanor, would you like a shower?" the nurse asks while raising an eyebrow to me.

"Does she need to stand?" I ask. But no, Ellie will lie in a tub while the water is run over her. "You can try," I say.

Ellie nods and the nurse is off again to gather help. While we wait, I bend to Ellie and touch her cheek, moving her hair across her forehead. I offer her some milkshake, which she takes in grateful sips. Two nurses return wheeling a bed frame fitted with a large, blue, soft-plastic tub. They lower the bedrails.

"Okay Eleanor, we're going to move you from the bed to the tub. You don't need to do anything, we'll do all of the work." The section of curtain facing the hall is pulled again and Ellie's brief is removed under her gown. With one nurse at Ellie's shoulders and one at her knees, they slowly inch her towards the edge of the bed then into the adjacent tub. They are steady and tender in their movements and I feel badly for becoming angry.

When Ellie is in the middle of the blue plastic tub she says, "Am I wet now? Am I in the water?" As the nurses begin pushing her out of the room and down the hall to the shower, a thin stream of pee comes from beneath Ellie and runs into a puddle in the corner of the tub.

I stand for a moment, watching, then return to the fresh, clean air.

Day 20

It's lunchtime in the great hall and it smells good, like gravy and potatoes and freshly-brewed coffee. Halfway down *Fir Grove* though, the aromas fade into a stale astringency. Ellie is sitting up in bed with a food tray in front of her, putting bits of cubed watermelon into her mouth. She chews the juice from them, then takes the soft remainder between her fingers and pulls it from her teeth, returning it to the bowl. I greet her and ask about her morning.

"They're organized here. I know exactly what's for breakfast but I can't help them with it."

"That's great, Ellie. It's nice to know what you're going to eat. What did they bring you?"

"Nothing!" Ellie says sharply. "They're border patrol." Her voice drops to a mutter. "Always patrolling."

The large bib has fallen to her stomach. There is a stain on the fabric of her gown. In between bites, she plays with a flap of skin that has loosened from her lip. My eyes keep wandering to it, watching her tongue come out between her wrinkled lips to wet it and move it around.

Two nurses come in, walking on either side of a woman using a walker. The lady with the walker has coloured her hair a dark copper. She's dressed in black slacks and a sequinned purple blouse. She wears a matching gold necklace and dangling bracelet.

All three of them enter the washroom. When the door is closed, I hear the woman say, "I look like an old lady." One nurse chortles back, "Oh no! No old ladies allowed here!" There is feigned laughter. They are in the bathroom for almost ten minutes before washing up and leaving back down the hall.

Outside the window, there is a bush with bright-red new growth. A prism hangs from the curtain rod. The light concentrates into a bright colourless centre then pours out, releasing itself into a dozen coloured streams. My eyes follow to where they dance on Ellie. Her arm is a patchwork of yellows, greens, blues, reds.

This is the brilliance of the prism: Gathered light made visible only through a host of faces that cast in extraordinary spectrums. A billion wavelengths of a billion tiny suns, perceptible only when embodied. This is life's own dazzling heart, best seen when broken open for and into the many. And when the sun goes down, what was partitioned is recollected into the glinting whole.

18

Pendulum:
A body suspended from a fixed point
so as to swing freely to and fro;
A device commonly used to regulate movement;
Something that easily alternates between opposites.

Year 4

Princess Margaret Hospital (PMH) stands in downtown Toronto, a few blocks from the provincial parliament buildings, the Eaton Centre and Yonge Street. It is one of the top-five cancer centres in the world, a massive enterprise with its own blood lab, pharmacy, library, gift shop, child and spiritual care services. The foyer opens to the first three of 18 floors. People ceaselessly arrive at every entrance from the subway, sidewalks, taxis, buses and shuttles. Patients come from all over Canada, and for those who can pay, from all over the world. Over 1000 patients come to PMH every day along with family members or friends.

We wait for an hour and a half on the day of my first appointment before being led into a small office. The doctor was forthcoming. "Because your cancer has shown both Hodgkins and non-Hodgkins cells, we need to re-examine your biopsies. If our pathologists believe your cancer is more Hodgkins, we will not do the transplant. Evidence shows that not only does it not work, but that it lowers the patient's quality of life to a degree that they wish they hadn't done it. Don't get your hopes up."

I felt crushed, angry and helpless. What bothered me most was his approach. He seemed habituated and hardened towards delivering this type of news, something I'm sure he had done hundreds of times. For me though, the patient, this was my first time and this was my life. We drove home and waited again.

Another month passed. I had another scan. This time, the scan showed less cancer, a sign that it was responding to the chemo. It was bittersweet. I was relieved it was responding, but knew it would be temporary without the transplant. We returned to PMH to find out the results of the biopsy.

This time, a different doctor spoke with us, accompanied by two interns. The doctor said that they had reviewed all of the information sent to them by Dr. Marian. "We agree," he said, "that the lymphoma looks more like non-Hodgkins than Hodgkins." I breathed out some of the tension I had been holding. Still, he was hesitant. "However, we are still unsure if we're going to give you the transplant. We don't usually use transplants for a new diagnosis."

Andrew and I looked at each other. New diagnosis? Exactly how many times did I need to relapse for this transplant to be approved?

"This is my third time with cancer," I said. The doctor raised an eyebrow and looked from one intern to the other. Now I understood. They had somehow missed this fact. There was only a moment of silence and then he said, "Well, in that case, you're in. No problem."

I learned that day why it is called *practicing medicine*. The brightest medical minds in the world, though well-intended and well-informed, sometimes get it wrong. I also learned that I am my own best advocate, that I don't need to feel shy or guilty about asking for clarification, questioning decisions, or making treatment suggestions. Had I not that day, I may be dead.

As I shook his hand on our way out, I asked the doctor, "What's the longest remission you've had from an allogenic transplant? He replied, "I just saw a man this morning who is 17 years cancer-free."

"Okay," I said. "See you in 20 years."

* * *

A date was set for my admission — August 20th, two months away. Enough time for another treatment and a few weeks to recover. Sophie came from France. We reminisced about a night in our teens when she snuck into my bedroom through our basement door. She had brought a chocolate cake from the convenience store refrigerator and we ate it on the bed before falling asleep side-by-side. One night, while I was in the hospital in Windsor, she showed up with the same refrigerated cake and two forks. We ate it together on the hospital bed and she spent the night with me, falling asleep upside down on the pullout chair. We laughed like when we were teenagers, talking about our friendship, now 25 years deep.

* * *

Throughout the summer, Andrew, Mom and I travelled regularly between Toronto and Windsor. There were still many steps to be completed before the transplant. I needed a chest x-ray, a bone marrow biopsy and blood work. My brother travelled from California to Toronto and also needed to undergo multiple tests before his stem cells would be harvested.

During this time, I began to work on stabilizing my internal energy, something which took considerable effort. I was experiencing a good deal of physical stress from the treatment and associated mental and emotional pain. I began to notice the ways in which my body held tension, my stomach tight and my energy either shutting down or scattering. I sometimes alternated between intense emotional pain and numbness.

A moment of fear could instantly refashion itself into elation and back again with a look from a doctor. My thoughts splayed themselves into projections about the future. I watched my mind race to the moment of my death and then linger on all of the sorrowful moments that would lead me there. Other times, I saw myself on a stage, having overcome cancer and giving motivational speeches. I let myself wonder if I would marry again or finish my theology degree or see my nieces and nephews in their adult bodies.

Appointments were heavy with anxiety. Seeing previous stem cell patients in the waiting room, some with red rashes on their faces, doubled over from GvHD of the gut or in wheelchairs, was frightening. My emotions and thoughts wanted to attach themselves to every person that passed, judging myself as healthier or sicker. I was also often indignant about the wait times — routinely one to three hours. I wondered if the doctor understood that I didn't have time to waste, that my time was just as valuable as theirs or more so, because it was limited.

Much of this stress arose from the continual unpredictability of the process. I was always waiting for things to normalize, for the externals to even out so I could return to a sense of inner equilibrium. Any sense of safety or trust was often quickly undermined by the outcomes of appointments, the comments of others, or a minor twinge in my body.

I soon became exhausted by this. My body, mind, and emotions were taut and weathered. I did not have energy to spare on endless anxiety. It wasn't just the negative that frayed me, either. Clinging solely to external positives also had to go. I began to understand that placing my sense of wellbeing on externals — even if they were favourable — would ultimately fail me. I needed to find and develop a place of security and refuge within myself.

Slowly, by noticing my reactions, I was able to take pause within them. Though the thoughts and feelings still occurred, my reactions became more tempered. I began to hold my energy rather than letting it scatter into attachment. By pausing, by holding my energy but not the event, something changed. The event that had so thoroughly just provoked me, passed. The emotions eased, my thoughts returned, and I settled. Over time, by watching this pattern repeat itself — the event, the intensity, the abating — I began to trust the process. *Event. Intense. Abate.* During these times I began to develop, or return to, a place of deep abiding.

The meditation and spiritual practices I had developed over the past years became a lifeline during these times. Time in meditation became the ground to which I could retreat; a place to be and to breath in silence and calm. This defused into the rest of my day, stabilizing my sense of identity and enabling me to be more fully present to my life.

It was a moment-to-moment practice to fully engage with my life while simultaneously cultivating non-attachment to its outcome. To engage when necessary; to let go when necessary. Soft, but not numb. Over time, though I still experienced emotional ups and downs, the swings became less extreme. No longer did the pendulum swing quite so wide and when it did, it took less time for the tipping ground to even out again.

* * *

I put the luggage in the trunk then drove to the pharmacy for some last minute items. I was picking Mom up at 9 a.m. so we could drive eastbound on the 401 towards Toronto. I would be admitted at 2 p.m. to Princess Margaret for paperwork and would begin treatment the following morning. On the way back from the pharmacy, my phone rang. I pulled into a parking lot and answered. It was Kristin, PMH's family counsellor.

"There's a spot on your lung, Anna. It showed up on your scan from last week. We just got the results. We're not sure what it is. It could be a fungus or a bacteria, but we need to treat it effectively before the transplant. If we don't, you may not be able to fight it when your immune system declines. It could become fatal."

The transplant, for now, was off. "How long?" I asked. They would admit someone else today in my place. It would be a month before another bed opened. Another month. In the long run, others assured me, a month won't make a difference if it offers the best chance for success. But for a mind that has counted on — fixated on — a given date, it was devastatingly difficult to adjust.

I went home and told Mom. We cried from the built-up anxiety and the wearing down of resources that were constantly being asked to change, adapt, adjust, accept. It was a weariness that came from alternating between states of adrenaline and exhaustion.

So, after giving tears their due, I decided that this time was grace and gravy and that I was going to make the best of it. Those days became glorious ones, glowing with the heat of the late summer and harboured by the knowledge of their certain end. I walked, ate well, got stronger, gave and received love.

In the course of this universe's long existence, and even in the span of my short life — a month, four weeks, 30 days — is so little.

19

Leak:
To release;
To enter or escape through an opening,
usually by a fault or mistake;
To become known despite efforts at concealment.

Year 4

That summer was the second time I felt death.

I was in the hospital for chemo; a different doctor was making rounds. Though my own doctor had said nothing about it, this doctor wanted to administer a dose of chemo into my spine. Regular chemotherapy could not break the blood-brain barrier and therefore provided no protection against the cancer spreading to my brain. A dose into the spine, the doctor told me, would travel directly to my brain and provide a safeguard against the cancer.

I felt uneasy, concerned about a needle entering my spine, but had met this doctor before and liked her. She asked if some residents could watch in order to learn the procedure. I consented, and four of them crowded into the small room. I laid on my side, slightly curled up so that the base of my spine was accessible.

The doctor felt around to locate the right spot. "You feel between the vertebrae at the base to find where the needle slips in," the doctor said. She pushed the needle tip in, moved it around, then pulled it back out without dispensing it. She tried again. Then again. I began to sweat, nervous now about her puncturing something unfixable in my back. Finally, she found the right location and emptied the syringe into my spine. Shaken, I went back to my room.

Within a few hours, I began to experience a terrible headache that continued to worsen. I asked for pain meds. They didn't help. I was told that it was a side effect of the injection and would soon subside. But it continued into the next day, and the next. The pain was so terrible that all I could do was lay in the bed with my eyes closed and the lights off. I asked Andrew to put a sign on the door that read NO VISITORS, though he and Mom sat beside me for hours. If I sat up and tried getting to the washroom, I would vomit from the pain. Only lying down seemed to ease it at all. All the while, my other chemo continued, along with the nurses' assurance that the headache would pass.

I was discharged without feeling any better. Finally, the home care nurse visited and confirmed that I had a persistent leak of spinal fluid into the epidural sac at the base of my spine. In order to stop the leak, the sac had to be 'patched' with a bit of my blood. I went back to the hospital and the sac was patched. Almost instantly, the headache stopped. The other chemo effects had mostly worn off so I immediately felt much better.

During that time, the pain bound me to bed. For most hours of the day, I laid as still as possible in a darkened room, mentally willing the pain to ease. Praying the pain would ease. I was unable to enjoy company, eat or open my eyes. One of the only thoughts I recall having during those days: *This is why people want to die.* My pain was debilitating but I hoped reversible. I didn't want to die, I wanted the pain to stop. But if this pain was accompanied by no chance of recovery, death would have been a release.

The body prepares us for death. When our bodies are young and strong, we can't imagine dying. It is too foreign from our daily physical experience. As we age or become ill, the body supplies us with a series of losses that soften our resistance to death.

The body slows, tires, weakens. The body is not able to maintain its previous pace, engage in the same activities it once found pleasurable, or continue in the roles it once enjoyed. These changes are often difficult to welcome and deserve the tender touch of our compassion. These changes are real and deserved to be grieved.

But if we continue to resist these changes, our mind and emotions become tangled in a sense of diminution and depletion. We see death and loss as errors in the system, things to be corrected rather than as integral parts of life. We not only become averse to our dying but hostile towards it (and then of course, to our own dying body). We fight it at all cost and the cost is this: When the body's need to die is strongly resisted, an internal crisis occurs. The person feels this opposition play out within themselves, causing a kind of psychic pain unrelieved by medication. A person is pulled unwillingly to their death.

For others, the spirit and psychology ready first. Sometimes seen in people of an advanced age, those who have tired after a long illness or who are in chronic pain, or in those who have simply found peace with their lives —

these folks speak of *being ready*. Curiously, the body itself may not be ready and this can be unsettling.

And still, there are people for whom there is a harmonic arising of the internal and external during their dying. It is not that the process of emotional upheaval or existential distress is avoided or absent. The feelings and thoughts around dying may be just as fierce. The difference may be in the acceptance of, and working with, these strong emotions, seeing them as both normal and necessary.

Rather than contracting around fear and pain, these forces are allowed to expand the heart, mind and body. There is a deep exhalation of control, fear and resistance. This is more than tolerance, perhaps even more than acceptance. It manifests as a *profound trust* that life and death are held by an overarching spirit of benevolence, whether natural law or spiritual love.

20

Needle:
A slender instrument used for introducing or removing material;
A thin pointer that indicates direction;
To deliberately antagonize.

Eleanor

Day 21

"Good morning Ellie!" I say as I come around the curtain. Ellie is sitting up in bed, her eyes fixed beyond the window. She turns to me and confusion crosses on her face.

"Are you alright?" I ask. Her face shifts.

"Of course I'm alright!" she answers. "I'm with you!" She holds up her hand and I grasp it in mine. Her hair has been combed and looks nice. I tell her so. She is ready to talk today. The first thing she asks: "How was your wedding?" I tell her that it was wonderful, that Andrew and I got married right here in town.

"We wanted to get married by the lake, but it poured rain, so we lit the wood stove and got married in the living room." I smile.

"Wonderful!" Ellie says. I wonder who she thinks I am today; a friend, a niece, a sister? It does not matter whose identity I borrow, as long as it is a comfort to Ellie.

A nurse comes in with a painkiller. Ellie's face screws up, cringes, and closes her eyes. While the nurse slowly empties the needle into Ellie's arm, she turns to me. I have the sense that, knowing Ellie has no family, she's curious about our relationship.

"Are you a friend from church?" the nurse asks.

"I'm from hospice," I say.

"Oh!" she says. She tells me that she's formally retired but back working casual shifts and thinking of stopping altogether when her nursing license is up for renewal in six months. Afterwards, she'd like to start volunteering. "How was the training?" she asks.

I tell her my opinion, that everyone can benefit from the training, seeing as how we will all die someday. I also tell her that my experiences volunteering have been both valuable and deeply satisfying. She looks down at the orange sherbet I've brought and the washcloth laid out.

"I feel badly," she says. "We just don't have the time." She slips the tip of the needle out of Ellie and wipes the site clean. Ellie opens her eyes and says, "Thank you."

"No," says the nurse. "Thank you." The nurse looks down into Ellie's face with such warmth that I say, "Looks like you're already doing hospice care." Before she leaves, she shares some of that smile with me.

I peel the lid from the sherbet and scoop a small amount on a spoon. Ellie takes the first bite, then fumbles for the handle. I place it in her hand and bring the cup close to her. It is a lot of work to get the slippery sherbet onto the spoon and through the air the distance to her mouth. The first piece slides off midway and falls to her chest. She tries again. There is a single-mindedness to her movements. Ellie's desire for autonomy is captured in this one, determined effort. This time, the spoon makes it to her mouth. She sighs as the cold hits her tongue.

"Will you have some soup with me?" she asks.

"I've had mine," I tell her. "I brought that one for you." Another nurse enters the room and walks over with an envelope.

"Are you Mrs. Davis?"

"Yes, I am!" Ellie is happy to be asked.

"I have mail for you." He puts an envelope down on her tray.

"Thank you!" Ellie calls as he walks out of the room. "Could you open it?" she asks, turning to me.

When I pull out the notice, I see it's from the RHA, the Regional Hospital Authority. It's an invoice for $3,500 for Ellie's stay in the hospital. I'm embarrassed by seeing something so personal of Ellie's. I have no idea as to her financial security and I don't want to upset her. I stare at it for a moment and then look up to see the spoon has dropped to Ellie's stomach and she is nodding off. I fold the notice back into the envelope and write on the outside. *Peg, this came while I was with Ellie. Not sure what to do with it. Thanks, Anna.* I place it on her night table. As I stand to leave, I wonder what automated system decided to send Ellie's financial statement to her death bed.

Day 22

Ellie sleeps while two men work to fix the mobility pulleys over the bed that is kitty-corner to hers. The men lay on the floor, sliding in and out under the bed to make sure the electrical is connected properly. I wonder what kind of germs live out their lives on these floors. The men talk loudly, making jokes as if they are alone. There is a kind of invisibility that surrounds Ellie and me. For them, this facility is their workplace, not someone's entire living room and bedroom and home.

One of the men uses a drill to open the electrical panel. He sets off an alarm that sirens off the walls. The men do not warn us and do not apologize. My eyes go wide and fly to Ellie, but somehow she's still asleep. At the best of times my ears are sensitive to noise but this is highly annoying.

It ends as Ellie's neighbour, the woman with the copper-coloured hair, walks into the room. She is wearing the same purple blouse and multiple bracelets and rings. In a place awash in blue cotton, it seems a dignity for her to dress her best, even if it's in the same blouse everyday. She stops at the end of Ellie's bed.

"What's her name?" she asks. I tell her that it's Eleanor.

"What's wrong with her?" This I avoid, instead asking if there is anything I can do for her. She makes her way to the edge of her bed across from Ellie's and sits down.

"Actually," she says, "would you scratch behind my shoulder for me? I can't reach it and it's really itchy." I walk over and lightly scratch the spot where she gestures. She begins to talk about a stream of things: the food, her family, her body's aches.

"How did I get here?" she asks in a voice that indicates that hers is not a question of mobility or of memory. It is not even about how she came to this long-term care facility in the first place. Hers seems a question of identity. How did I get here — to the end of my life, alone and aged, living here? How did I become this — this old lady in the mirror

— from the person I always considered myself to be? It's a question about the mystery of life. It's a question about an itch she cannot reach.

"There. How is that?" I ask after a few minutes.

"Fine. Better. Thank you. I know I shouldn't be keeping you."

"That's okay," I say, returning to sit by Ellie. A few minutes later, the woman takes a ruler from her nightstand and moves it under the back of her shirt, scratching desperately for relief.

Day 23

It's a warm, windy day. I've passed two of Ellie's roommates in the great hall. One is the lady in the purple shirt, who is eating breakfast. The other is the 90-year-old. She looks at me with eyes empty of recognition. Ellie's third roommate I've never seen, but I know lives there because of the pictures hanging above the bed and the handwritten sign that reads: *The family will do her laundry.*

The room is dark, except for the overhead lamp.
Ellie is awake and has a straw in her mouth, sipping right from the large carafe in front of her. Instead of water, the carafe has been filled with chocolate nutritional shake and ice.

"What have you got there?" I ask her, smiling. She doesn't miss a beat.

"A piña colada." She winks. I laugh, turning to put my bag down on the chair. When I turn back, Ellie eyes are drooping. I am again surprised by the clarity with which the forces of life and death are visible. I ask her if she would like me to wash her face.

"Yes."

I pull a clean cloth from the linen cart outside of the room and run it under cool water. I begin at her forehead, slowly moving down her temples and across her cheeks. I let the cloth linger for a moment on each of her closed eyelids. I clean across her mouth. I freshen the cloth again and lay it on her arm, gently moving it down to her hands and between her fingers. Ellie sighs. When I have finished both arms, I pick up the comb and move it though her soft hair, smoothing it around her face. I squeeze a little moisturizer onto her lips.

A few quiet minutes pass then Ellie says, "I'm cold." I pull the blankets up and tuck them around her. I rub her arms to warm her. Her eyes close again. I move the chair beside her, sit down, and watch her breathe. Her face is soft. Most of my time with Ellie has simply been spent witnessing her; the twitches and aches of her body, the delicate area of skin where the needle slips in, the memories and concerns that stir and surface in the last weeks of a life. Water, touch, warmth, breath.

These are the small and significant things that we build our lives around. This is what we do when we love someone. It's what lovers do, and long-time friends do, and what parents do for their children. We become the eyes and ears and hands that take in, hold, and affirm another's life. I cannot stop Ellie's dying. What I can do is to be a faithful witness to the certainty that she, her life and her death, are worthy of witnessing. This is the gift we can give to each other.

21

Isolate:
To quarantine;
To select from among others;
To separate so as to obtain purity.

Year 4

There were eight rooms on the 14th floor isolation ward. Locked doors, filtered air. No plants allowed. No children. No one remotely unwell, except for the patients. The spot on my lung had disappeared with antibiotics and here I was, supplied with a month's worth of clothes and prayers. My room was directly across from the nurses desk, though none of the rooms were very far.

The room was large though plain, painted in off-white. Each room had a stationary bike. The lead doctor was researching how exercise affected recovery time. I also had my own bathroom with a shower and sitz bath for if — when — I had prolonged diarrhea. A chart was drawn on the white board with the days of the week and blood marker headings: RBC (red blood cells), WBC (white blood cells), platelets. My blood would be taken and recorded each day to monitor what was happening on a cellular level. The best part of the room was the big west-facing window with a view of the city and Lake Ontario. Thank God for that window.

My first hour after finishing the paperwork, I prioritized: I decorated. On the cork board went a photo collage of family and friends. The blue-and-yellow prayer quilt I was given after my first diagnosis — the one with prayers knotted into the yarn ends — went on the single bed. On the ceiling above the bed I taped quotes that had become important to me. They went on the ceiling because I knew that's where I'd see them, lying in bed for days. I knew from experience that reading a book or watching a movie would, at some point, become too difficult. I needed a few, simple mantras for when my attention couldn't hold anything more.

Be still and know that I Am God.[2]

On my last appointment before being admitted, I had asked the lead doctor, "What can I do for myself during this time?" He replied, "Do me a favour. Don't be a patient. Do as much for yourself as you can. Get up, walk, shower, try to eat. Do what you can." He told me about a patient who had walked 80 laps around the unit while there. I became determined to do more. Walking was my *thing*.

So outside of my door went a piece of paper titled *Walking Log* with a pen taped to it, so I could easily record my laps. In the centre of my door went a picture of me — healthy, haired, smiling me — with *Anna* over top of it. Underneath it read, *Turn up the Joy.*

I wanted to remind the doctors, nurses, chaplains and lab staff who came through that door that it was a real

2 Psalm 46:10.

person they were tending, not an illness. I especially wanted them to be reminded when all that seemed to lay in the bed was a pale, weakened body. I wanted them to see the vibrancy that lay resting but ready in my heart. I wanted them to be invested in helping this vibrancy to once again inhabit my body.

Be still and know that I Am.

The first of the four weeks was for daily chemotherapy. Because my blood counts would not drop until into the second week, I was able to leave the hospital for a few hours each day between treatments. I got up early on those mornings, taking the elevators down to the ground floor and walking out onto the busy streets of Toronto. Autumn was arriving and the air smelled of the time in-between life and death. I took it all into me, breath after breath. At night, Andrew and I would walk again, the city perpetually alive with lights and sounds and people. And, while hooked up to the chemo I walked around the ward, making tally ticks after each lap.

This first week came with a remarkable sense of delight. The anticipatory waiting of the last few months had given way to the actuality of the transplant. I felt healthy and strong and hopeful. Every person, every particle, seemed to shimmer with life. I had a heightened sense of pleasure that came through my senses. Colour, warmth, light, voice, taste, and breath. The simple in-and-out of my breath, happening over 20,000 times a day without my conscious awareness. My tether to life.

At the end of the first week came the day in which I would have my first-ever radiation treatment. Rather than be targeted to a specific area, the radiation would be delivered to my entire body. It was intended to kill any remaining cancer cells and further suppress my immune system for transplant. Out of all of the treatments I have had, this was the one in which I experienced the greatest sense of vulnerability.

I was brought to the radiation unit where I changed into a gown. Leaving my clothes behind, I was led into a room emptied of everything but — not a bed, but a tray — on which to lie. After positioning me, the tech left the room. The door closed and a sign above it lit up. *Caution: Radioactivity. Do not enter.* I laid there alone and cold. The room filled with radiation and surrounded me, then permeated the boundary of my skin and settled in my cells.

Be still and know.

Then began the decline. The chemo and radiation did their work, slowing killing off my cells. I began to feel tired and sick, sleeping more and more. But I had done this before and could still hold some conversation and watch movies.

Then, Day Zero arrived — the day when I would be given my brother's stem cells. From here, days would be counted as +1, +2, +3 and on from the transplant date. Tom had donated his stem cells in the summer and they had been kept frozen. The morning of the transplant, the slow thawing began. It was a small bag, about the quantity of a can of pop. The preservative smelled like tomato soup.

The room was crowded. Andrew, my mom and aunt, the hospital chaplain, the doctor and several nurses came in and out of the room. Part of the protocol was that I would be given Ativan beforehand. I was told that some patients get quite nervous or anxious at the time when the donor cells are infused and Ativan is given in advance to prevent this. I had never taken Ativan and felt hesitant about taking it without knowing what effect it would have on me. Still, the nurses insisted.

The plan was that shortly after being given the Ativan, Tom's cells would be brought to the room and infused over about 10 minutes. While the cells were flowing, Mom would FaceTime Tom so that I could talk to him and he could be a part of the process. Mom would video the whole thing.

The video shows this: I am sitting in bed with the iPad on my lap. My brother is on the screen, talking. I am trying to say something but my words keep slurring. The iPad is falling over; I can't hold it up. He keeps asking me, "Are you okay?"

The video makes me feel sick when I watch it, I am so out of it. I woke up hours later, having missed the entire experience. I felt angry and invaded. The transplant was something I had greatly prepared for mentally, emotionally and spiritually. I felt that my choice to be conscious throughout it had been taken away. Everyone else in the room had been allowed to fully experience the miracle I felt the transplant was — even if it also brought them tears, relief, hope or anxiety. But for me, the patient — the person it was actually taking place *in and for* — that choice had been taken away in fear that I would become too distressed.

Be still.

In the early hours of each morning, my blood was drawn while I lay half-asleep. Each day revolved around the white board, as we waited for the results to be filled in. Tom's stem cells needed time to travel to my bones, re-seed the marrow and mature before they could be released into my blood stream to bring my immunity back up. During this time — two to three weeks — my blood cell counts hovered at virtually undetectable levels. I started taking antibiotics to prevent opportunistic infections, just one of the drugs that I would continue for an entire year.

Next, I entered a time for which there is little description. I developed an open sore in my throat. I had already stopped eating but the sore was so painful that swallowing became difficult. I was put on a morphine drip for four days. Andrew had been coming to the hospital each day, but had caught a cold and could not visit. During those long days, I would briefly open my eyes when Mom arrived in the morning, then once more when she touched my arm to say goodbye. "You just got here," I would mumble, before realizing that seven hours had passed.

I often wonder where I was during that time of strange sleep. Where did I go? My body was so utterly weighted to the bed but the rest of me — the efforts, opinions, actions of Anna — existed only in memory.

It was as if I was cloistered in a warm winter; silent and suspended in a white slumber. Undocumented time; unpigmented space. Around me, the nurses kept me alive, adding or taking away things to protect me. And I was sheltered by the constant companionship of my loved ones who, near and far, shaped themselves into a ring of protection around me. My normal defences against the divine — my sense of a separate identity, my perpetual thoughts and actions — dropped away. Never, since I was a child, had I been so vulnerable and therefore, so open. Taking its opportunity, the divine drew closer to me then perhaps ever before.

You were with me even when I wasn't with myself. When I awoke, for just moments at a time, I tried to think of You. To pray or meditate as I have learned. But I was too exhausted for presence of mind. Though I had little awareness of it, still I breathed. This is faithfulness; not mine, but Yours.

Sometimes at night, I turned my head towards the window. Suspended 14 storeys above the earth, I hovered there while the beautiful world went on below. The night sky shimmered around me with all manner of light; a twinkling womb. In these ways, it was never truly dark.

Be.

* * *

Finally, two weeks after the transplant and three weeks into my stay at PMH, the nurse came in, smiling. My blood levels had once again reached detectable levels. Tom's cells were engrafting. Full engraftment would take some time, but this was a very positive step. The sore in my throat healed, and with my increasing blood counts, my energy and appetite slowly returned. I needed to be eating, drinking and walking at least moderately to be discharged. I started my laps again, though could now only complete one loop at a time before returning to my bed to rest. The IV fluids were decreased. Ten days later, one month after arriving, I was discharged. Stepping out into the world, after being inside an isolation ward for one month, was both exhilarating and overwhelming.

I was discharged to the Lodge, PMH's accommodations for out-of-town patients. Mom had been staying there and now the two of us would remain there together for at least a month. Twice a week we would take the shuttle to the hospital for blood work and appointments where I was monitored for signs of infection and GvHD.

Though the Lodge wasn't home, after weeks spent on an isolation ward, it seemed luxurious. Our days at the Lodge were rhythmed with a deep indulgence in simplicity. Warm oatmeal with milk; seedy jam on brown toast. We read the newspaper over coffee, worked a puzzle, took afternoon naps. I walked the halls, going up the stairs on one side of the building, crossing the length of the hall and returning down the stairs on the other side. There was an exercise room and I spent time stretching and doing light weights and cardio. I became engrossed in cooking shows, watching episode after episode of plates piled with burgers, pastas and desserts. I needed nourishment and helpings filled with comfort. Slowly, all of us — Andrew, Mom and me — limbered from the rigidity of surviving. We softened and became a little more satiated.

In the last week of November, after two and a half months in Toronto, the doctors prepared me to return home. I would still need to attend regular appointments, but no longer needed to live within a 30-minute commute of the hospital.

I had many conflicting feelings about going home. Though going home healthy had been my goal for so long, home now seemed light-years away. I had changed during the last months, not only because of what my body had been through, but because of the people I had met and what we had witnessed happening in and to one other.

One isolation ward. One month. Eight patients. A lifetime. I did not yet have the words or energy to describe my experiences, something I knew people would be curious about. I felt so changed that I wondered how I would ever adjust to 'normal' life again. I felt very tender emotionally and wanted to stay swaddled in the soft intimacy of just the three of us.

In early December, Mom and I said goodbye to Andrew, who would stay in Toronto for a few more weeks, and drove towards home. There, a new tenderness and comfort met us, and assured me that all would be well. It was healing to lie on the familiar couch cushions, to hold my favourite mug, to have the fields and the sky back in my field of vision. My anxiety about what to say to visitors dissolved when I saw them, these friends who were with me all along.

Christmas came, a snowy, cozy time filled with tradition and cheer. As I returned home, a new sense of home was returned to me. The year came to an end.

22

Wake:
To rouse from sleep;
The track left by a moving body;
A gathering associated with death.

Eleanor; Dad

Day 24

It's a sleepy Sunday morning at Woodhaven. Residents linger over plates of eggs and cups of coffee in the Great Room. I've come mid-morning since I'm leaving at noon for a two-day sightseeing trip with Andrew and our friends who are visiting from Ontario.

Ellie is alone in the room, asleep in bed. I quietly move the chair into the sun streaming in from the window. I sit down, tilt my face to the warmth and close my eyes.

Soon, I hear Ellie's legs move against the sheets. I watch her face in the moment just before she opens her eyes. When she does, she smiles softly and works to sit up in bed.

"Good morning Ellie," I say.

"Good morning," Ellie says. There's a long pause and then, "How are your mom and dad?" I look at her, my head jerking in surprise. I tell her that I just journaled about my dad that morning.

Though it felt awful at the time, Debbie's honesty about Dad's condition was a gift. Instead of waiting for Father's Day as planned, my older brother immediately brought his family to see Dad. Had they waited, they would not have seen Dad alive again. Debbie was right; Dad died within two-and-a-half weeks of being admitted to the hospital.

His wake was held on Father's Day. The room at the funeral home was filled with elements of Dad's life — picture boards of him at stages throughout his life, many relatives and friends, and even his body. Still, it was a hollow day, a vast and endless day. Before the casket was closed and taken to the church, Dad's wedding band was removed and given to Mom.

I remember little of the service. I do recall the kindly old priest turning to our family seated in the front pew and saying, *And now, I'm going to speak to the family.* But what did he say? All I saw was the day two years before when Dad had walked me down this same aisle. We had paused there, in the heart of this church where his body now lay, before he kissed me. The skin of our living faces had touched for just a moment.

When the service concluded, I stood with my brothers and sisters and we surrounded Dad's casket. From the time of our births Dad had bent, picked up, and carried each of us through the moments of our lives; through our mistakes, when we fell or fell asleep. Now was our time to do the same for him, our only father.

We each clasped the small corner of this sorrow that we could bear. We bent, held on, and only together, lifted him. Surrounded by the many who loved him, we carried Dad from the church's heart down the steps and into the hearse. This is what love does. It bears you from altar to altar.

Instead of driving to the cemetery, we climbed into a limo and drove to the luncheon while Dad's body went to the funeral home to be incinerated. When Dad died, he became the first person I knew to choose cremation over burial. While eating crustless sandwiches and bright green coleslaw, I pictured Dad lying on a large long-handled pizza peel, slowly sliding into a wood-burning oven raging with fire.

A few days later, Dad's body was returned to us in seven white, gold-rimmed containers. There were six small ones inscribed with *Dad*, and a large one with *Mike* for Mom. It seemed like a lot of material for just my dad. Of course, Dad had not been on a pizza peel, but in the coffin when he was cremated. My little jar held both.

In that first year after Dad's death, I learned about the degree of pain a body could hold and still live. At times, I sobbed until I felt there was nothing left inside of me, then I sobbed some more. I needed to get it out of my body. I felt as though it might kill me otherwise. I bit the insides of my mouth, pressed my palms to my eyes and screamed, trying to externalize the pain.

When the pain became great, I would hold the little jar close to me. Sometimes, I would take the lid off and dip my fingers into the ash, rubbing it into my palms. I wondered what part of him I had — a fingernail, a bone? I had an urge to put some in my mouth, to swallow the ash and have him flow through my blood, inseparable from me forever.

I used to think it was strange that people kept remnants of burnt bodies in their homes, but now I understood.

That little jar gave me something of my dad's real, physical presence to keep in a way that a burial wouldn't have. It was a consolation to have something of him to touch, some tangible evidence of his existence.

I understood then that *to rend* is primarily an inner searing, something that first happens on a deep, interior level. In the moment of Dad's death, a hot blade pressed itself into me, splitting open the flesh of my life, spilling it out into a raw, mangled mess. Everything I knew or thought I knew, everything I was or was becoming, everything I thought had been important and no longer was, became subject to this laceration. I was disemboweled of my illusions of permanence and perfection. I felt my life — and my family's life — mutilated. *To rend* is a branding of the soul. Pulling hair, tearing clothes and wailing are merely the insignia.

When Dad died, all time became measured against that day. Life was delineated between *Before Dad* and *After Dad*. Dad's death gave other life events either a strange muteness or an unusual potency. Things that previously seemed crucial to spend time on no longer held interest for me. Then once, at the end of a hot August two months after Dad died, I was loading groceries into my trunk. My fingers curled around a basket of Ontario peaches and I was suddenly crying. I was pulled into a scene from years before; a dusty county road, an old car filled with kids, a father pulling out a few dollars at a roadside stand. The fuzzy face of a peach, releasing its sticky juice on my lips.

During that time someone told me: *One day, after some time passes, you'll wake up in the morning and realize that you didn't think of him the previous day. When that day comes, be gentle with yourself.* This irritated me greatly. Dad's death felt so encompassing that a day like that seemed both undesirable and implausible.

But as the circle of time widened away from his death, it felt like Dad, the clarity of him, was drawn from me, too. On the one-year anniversary of his death, I took the day off of work. My family and I went out to the field where his memorial tree was planted. We dug a small garden around it, planting a rose bush and an Irish flag into the soil. From one of the tree's thin branches, we hung a small plaque engraved with a quote from St. Augustine:

Restless 'til I rest in Thee

After that, I began to measure time in months rather than in days from his death and the pain eased.

Then, the circle of time reached some outer arc and began to bow back, returning Dad to me in new ways. I found in moments of meditation that Dad was present. Meditation allowed me to enter into aspects of relationship with Dad that I didn't have access to while he was alive. We were both freed of the constraints of our previous relationship and became available to one another in new ways. I could listen to and see him as *himself*, not only as my father. I asked him for guidance and for help. I went back to moments between us that needed healing.

Once, I went back to the night I was called to the hospital by my siblings. That night, when Mom began speaking those awful words about Dad's condition and my siblings broke down crying around him, I couldn't look my father in his eyes. All I could say was, "No. No. That's ridiculous." I was so afraid, but my face showed anger. It was just two weeks before his death.

During meditation, when I returned to this night and Mom delivers the news, I lift my eyes in love to each of my siblings and reach my hands to them. We form a circle around Dad and I bend to him and look into his face. Then all the love inside of us wells up, overflows and heaps itself upon him. I say, *It's okay Dad. You'll always be with us.* And though we are crying, the heat of our bodies and our love encircles Dad, and he looks up from the bed to see that this is indeed so. He smiles and lays back, deeply assured.

And I realize that part of what I have been doing, in this place and in this time with Ellie, is working out my own losses. I'm careful about tending to my losses through journaling, rituals, talking and crying. But grief can be wild and wide. Ellie's acceptance of death has rounded out my grief, stabilizing it. In this hallowed space between us, spirit-birds slip from their perch in my heart and circled overhead, filling the space with their fluttering wings.

"Mike Byrne," I say aloud. *Mike Byrne.* I'm hoping she'll remember. I'm hoping she'll remember his name when she goes to where he may be. Ellie nods at me. She closes her eyes again. In her sleep, Ellie groans and kicks her legs under the sheets, restless like she's caught in a bad dream. She awakens, hands rigid in the air, fingers splayed. I grasp them in my own.

"Are you okay?" I ask.

"No. No." Her eyes close again to the dream.

I begin to hum. There is no particular tune, just a soft, low vibration moving through my flesh and out into the open air to be taken up by her. I think of the times in my life when I have been hummed or sung to, and of the nieces and nephews I sing to now. An instinctive use of breath to soothe and settle. Ellie quiets. I hum and hum and hum. Later, on my way to the door, Ellie awakens once more.

"And where," she asks, "is my mother?"

23

Trip:
To catch against something and stumble;
To trigger a mechanism;
To make a journey.

Year 5

In January, Andrew and I returned to Toronto for a check-up with the hospital. We decided to stay a few extra days to attend a live music event. Every morning after breakfast we went to the gym, then would spend a few hours writing. Feeling the ache of my muscles at night, having acoustic guitar music fill my ears, having my pen to paper once more, all told me that I was alive. I had survived. Though full recovery was predicted to take a year, my energy had returned in the last month and I already felt stronger and also, happier.

Then, while back home in February, I began to have stomach pains. It began as mild discomfort and steadily grew worse. After two days, I called Dr. Marian. She told me to come directly to the hospital to see her, that I was likely beginning to experience graft-versus-host disease. After looking at my vital signs and recent blood work, she explained the benefits and drawbacks of controlling the GvHD with steroids.

"The steroids will decrease the GvHD, but it will also suppress the grafting process, the graft-vs-lymphoma effect. What I'm most concerned about is dehydration." The risk was that if the GvHD worsened, it could cause hemorrhaging. After discussing it, we decided to wait and see what the GvHD would do. If it worsened, I could quickly begin steroids, but for now, I would drink extra fluids and hope it settled down on its own. I also called the clinic at PMH to let them know. They advised that if it worsened, I return to Toronto immediately.

Over the next day or so, the symptoms intensified. Though I couldn't eat, the whole of my digestive tract seemed inflamed with cramping and painful gas. I began having terrible diarrhea. I lay in the recliner by the window trying to sleep. Finally, it was bad enough that I asked Andrew to drive me to Toronto.

Back at PMH, I was started on prednisone, an oral steroid that would suppress my immune system and the GvHD. I was readmitted to the Lodge. My energy plummeted and I became weak again. Every morning until the GvHD subsided, Andrew and I took the shuttle from the Lodge to the hospital where I received IV hydration, potassium and magnesium.

Within a week, the prednisone began to work and I started to feel better. As soon as my symptoms were under control, the doctors began decreasing the dose of prednisone. Prednisone is a powerful drug that does its work well. It also comes with the possibility of serious side effects including heart failure, anaphylaxis, and a range of psychiatric reactions like depression and psychosis. One of the effects I got was 'moon face', in which my cheeks grew rounder, shaping my face into a circle, which looked funny on my thin body. In the end, it took me six months to be weaned from prednisone.

After a few weeks, we returned to Windsor. With the help of the drugs, life went on. In March I celebrated my 36th birthday. I took a seminary course in Detroit. At the end of June, Tom asked if I would go on a road trip with him as he drove from Ohio, where they had lived for a year, back to California. I wanted so badly to go, but was nervous as I was nearing the end of the prednisone and feared withdrawal symptoms. I was also concerned that without the prednisone, the GvHD would return. The doctors encouraged me to go, keeping my dose at a low, consistent level until I returned. They also suggested that it was a good time to have my central line removed.

The implantation of different ports and central lines — three over the course of the last few years — were always accompanied by feelings of disappointment and sadness as they signalled the need for long-term chemotherapy treatment. I understood their necessity and reluctantly consented to their place in my body. But then, when their function had been served and the time came to remove them, other feelings arose. The ports came to represent a sense of safety, however illogical. I felt that removing them would be to tempt fate, that as soon as they came out, I'd need them again.

My aunt offered to accompany me to the port removal appointment. The procedure would be done at the PMH clinic under local anesthetic and was scheduled to only take a few minutes. I knew from the past that a small slit would be made in my skin and with a few good tugs by the doctors, the line would loosen from my vein and the whole thing would come out.

But after administering the anesthetic and making the cut, the line wouldn't loosen. It seemed it had been stitched in along a vein and that my tissue had grown over the stitches. After a few unsuccessful attempts, the doctor called in a colleague and together they tried everything from using a small scalpel, to wiggling it back and forth, to yanking on it quite strongly. It was a very strange sensation to have someone hovering above me, their hand in my chest, pulling very hard but not being able to feel anything.

More time passed. I asked for one of them to please let my aunt, who was waiting in the hall, know what was happening. Finally, they called in the lead doctor. It seemed quite embarrassing for them. The doctor put on gloves and began. He also was having difficulty. I saw water pour out onto the floor and I couldn't figure out what it was. Finally, the line loosened and came free. I think they were relieved as much as I was.

One of the doctors began patching me up while the other one cleaned the area. "Oh," said the youngest doctor, "there's water on the floor." The lead doctor looked down and said, "Sorry...that was me. I was sweating." The sweat had actually poured out of his gloves. An hour and a half had passed. I felt emotionally and physically exhausted. But it was over and the port was out.

I took that drive with Tom, crossing 10 states in three days, taking turns driving, talking about our childhood memories, listening to music and watching the landscape pass around us. Andrew flew to California to meet us when we arrived and we spent a few days helping my brother and his family to unpack. Then Andrew and I took the commuter train up to San Francisco for two nights. We watched the Blue Jays play the Giants, had lunch on the wharf and walked the winding streets. It was ordinary and it was astonishing.

* * *

In 10 years, will I still cry if I come to PMH?

I wondered this as I sat in the clinic waiting room, my eyelashes holding water before they formed into drops. I was approaching my one-year post-transplant appointment. There was a man I recognized from the 14th floor, whose name I couldn't remember. His transplant had been a day before mine. I'd seen him here during past appointments. Following the transplant he had GvHD of the gut, a lung infection and then a virus that made him bed-bound. He'd spent the better part of six months in the hospital and was now practicing how to stand.

My own appointment was a happy one. Prednisone done! Bone protector medication done! One more month and the three antibiotics would finish.

* * *

Tom called and asked me this question: *You are going on a trip and you won't know the destination until you arrive. You have 10 minutes to pack five things. What do you bring?* I listed granola with dark chocolate, water, a paper and a pen and an envelop addressed to Tom, to send him the thoughts I write while on the trip. *Ok,* he said, *explain why you chose these.*

Well, I figure that if I go to either the tundra or the desert, I won't be able to pack enough to survive for long, so I might as well make it meaningful. I brought the pen and paper to leave a record, and the granola for enjoyment.

There was a pause, then: *So, you worked from the assumption that you would be going to one of two of the most uninhabitable places on earth and that you would only live a few days. You didn't expect anything fun or positive. You had no choice in going, assumed it was a test of survival, and that you had at most, a few days to live.*

It hadn't crossed my mind that it might be something wonderful or the trip of my dreams, only that it would be a challenge I must face. As such, I thought that I better hunker down and do something worthwhile and lasting. Why did I expect to die?

Why? said Tom. *Maybe because you've been fighting for your life for the last five years?*

* * *

Most days, I woke feeling grateful. I thought about the previous year, waking in the hospital and going to sleep there, alone in the white stuffy room with artificial lights that never went out.

Life was simple and happy. Like the day Andrew and I spent together in the apartment, writing, hanging pictures, cleaning our sacred space, having tea and chocolate. Then, in the afternoon, a visit to a coffee shop and more writing; he in the margins of a magazine and me, working on my seminary portfolio. Rain. Dinner. Magnetic poetry on the side of the refrigerator. Reading on the couch, listening to the thunder and lightening roll in. And Andrew turning to me at the end of the day, after all of this and saying, *I just want to hang out with you.*

On the one-year anniversary of the transplant, Andrew took a picture of me standing under the magnolia tree outside of the apartment. I held a sign that read *One Year.* My heart and being felt so full, so joyous, so ready to crack open with love. I laughed out loud and fought the urge to yell *I love you!* to everyone who passed, to somehow liberate the abundance I felt within me.

If you were to look down at me from the sky, you might see a million streams of coloured light bursting from my centre like confetti. *I am alive. We did it together.*

* * *

My one-year followup included another chest X-ray and blood work. I went to see the doctor who had found the spot on my lung a year ago which caused the transplant delay.

He came into the office where I was waiting and brought up the X-ray image on the computer, turning the screen towards me. "The spot from last year is gone," he said. "I'm so sorry, but there is something new showing."

"Ok," I said. "What could it be? Something like the infection last year?" I didn't feel panicked, given that the spot last year was related to my low immune system, something I still had. I didn't even worry when he abruptly stood and gestured me to follow him. "I'm going to try and catch the lab before it closes." Then, he actually took off running down the hall towards the lab, jumping *through* a silk tree as he rounded a corner out of sight.

I turned towards Andrew as we followed and said, "Either he's a very thorough doctor or I'm sick." The doctor decided that I would begin taking more antibiotics and antifungals to see if they helped. I felt fine otherwise, so we would wait a month and then redo the X-ray.

In October, the X-ray showed that the spot had continued to grow. The doctor speculated that perhaps I had picked up a rare infection from my road trip through the U.S. with Tom. The drugs were switched again. I had a bronchial washing, a procedure where I gargled with throat-numbing jelly and was then sedated. A scope was inserted down my throat and a saline solution flushed into my lungs then pulled back out for testing. Nothing significant appeared in the sample analysis. Around the same time, I started waking up with night sweats. My moods started to become unpredictable; I easily became teary. All of these, the doctors said, could be related to either the infection or the drugs.

I made a suggestion to my PMH doctors. "Why don't we do a full body CT scan and then we'll know if there's any other spots in my body?" They agreed. The scan came back negative for cancer. Whatever was happening, I felt confident that I could handle it because *at least it wasn't cancer.*

Another month passed and in November, I repeated the chest X-ray again. The spot had grown and was now 4 cm by 4 cm. It was time for a biopsy. When I met with the surgeon he told me, "If I'm going to go into your lung for a biopsy, I would just prefer to remove the spot." I agreed. I would be admitted for surgery in mid-December at Toronto General. The surgeon would remove an extra 1 cm around the spot in order to contain it.

I woke up after the surgery with a tube between two of my ribs that was draining fluid from my lung into a container next to the bed. Mom and Andrew were there. The doctor came in and said that the surgery had gone as planned and he believed that he had removed all of the tissue. He said, "I looked at the sample. I haven't seen anything like it before. I'm not sure what it is, but I don't think it's cancer." I fell back asleep.

I stayed three days, until I was walking a bit and didn't need many painkillers. The results of the biopsy would take a few weeks and so we went home for the holidays. Andrew and I became mall-walkers for a season, heading out each morning to walk among the mostly-retired seniors. We had a wonderful Christmas and I recovered quickly.

On January 6th, my brothers and sisters who had been visiting for the holidays either flew home or returned to work and school. It was Dad's birthday. It would have been his 80th. There was a heavy snowfall over night and Andrew and I woke early, put on our boots and jackets and went to a nearby nature park to walk. We were the first there that morning, everything fresh and flawless.

I called the nurse practitioner at PMH afterwards. *Just checking in. It's been 3 weeks and we haven't heard anything.*

That's probably good news. If they found something, you likely would have heard immediately. Hmm. I'm checking the computer and it looks like it will be ready tomorrow. I'll call you in the morning when I have it.

24

Vigil:
The act of keeping awake at times when sleep is customary;
A period of time to stay in place;
To watch and wait.

Eleanor

Day 25

We wake at 4 a.m. to drop our friends at the airport to catch their flight home, then arrive at my brother's early to watch the kids. Five hours later, we're home for lunch and naps. By 3 p.m., I'm rested and decide to run a few errands and then head to Woodhaven.

It's 3:40 p.m. when I arrive at the door to Ellie's room. The curtain is open. The space on the left side of the room near the window is empty. Ellie is gone and so is the bed. Without them, the space looks enormous. I stand there for a minute, then check the outside of the door. Ellie's name plate is still there. *She must be alive.*

Back at the nurses' desk I simply ask, "Eleanor Davis?" One of the nurses stands and walks towards me, pointing to a door across from the nurses' station.

"We moved her to the family room." She pushes open the door. The room inside is large and cozy. One wall is windowed with a private door that opens to the garden. There is a kitchenette with wood cabinets and enough sitting room for a fair-sized group of people. On the couch closest to Ellie, Peg sits reading a book.

"Peg!" I say, "I was hoping to see you."

"Me too," says Peg. "Come in."

I turn to Ellie, asleep in bed. There is a noticeable change in her breathing. Her chest rises hard with each inhale, then deflates wet, gurgling air. This, I know, is the *death rattle*. As I have done each time we're together, I bend down, touch her arm and say, "Hiya Ellie. It's Anna." I stay like that for several moments, my face close to hers. Just staying close to Ellie.

"When did they move her?" I turn back to Peg.

"Yesterday, when she began breathing like this. At first they didn't want to move her. Didn't want her to die alone. But the sound is distressing to others. I've been sitting here most of the day, but at lunch I had to leave. I just couldn't listen to it while I ate. In all my years as a nurse little bothered me, but this — phlegm — I've always had trouble with." The rattle is a laboured, sticky burble emitted from Ellie's throat as air passes through the accumulated fluid in her lungs.

As Peg tells me that Ellie has not awakened today, a nurse comes in and administers a shot to Ellie. After she leaves, Peg tells me the name of the drug and that it's meant to dry up the phlegm.

"I'm skeptical," she says, "since the last two doses haven't worked." We sit to talk. I tell Peg about my visit with Ellie just a few days ago, when she ate ice cream and joked about piña coladas. I confess my conflicted feelings about not visiting yesterday, but that we had company staying with us.

"You gotta live," Peg says. We chat about the highlights of Vancouver Island: Cathedral Grove, Mount Washington, Tofino. I ask whether she will be called when Ellie dies.

"Yes, my number's on file," she says. "I hope so." I tell her that if possible, I'd like to be called, too. Our conversation shifts to Peg's time as a nurse, working on intensive care units in both Canada and the United States. It was challenging work that she loved right up until her last year when administrative changes helped her decide to retire. "The best decision I've ever made," Peg says.

I tell her what a benefit it's been to have her here, knowing the medical protocol and how to advocate for Ellie's needs, especially in the absence of any family.

"Did you get used to it?" I ask. "Seeing people die?" Peg opens her mouth to respond, then stops. Ellie's breathing has changed. We stand, Peg moving to one side of Ellie and grasping her hand, while I do the same on the other.

"Well, the drug is working," Peg says. Ellie's breathing, though still difficult, has begun to dry up. Peg holds two fingers on Ellie's wrist for a minute. "I can't find a pulse. It's too weak. It won't be long now."

I picture myself brewing a pot of coffee in the wood kitchenette while the sky grows dark and the hallways grow quiet. In my mind, I watch myself sitting the night with Ellie, holding her hand. I'm tired, but Peg's been here all day and I don't want Ellie to be alone.

The last night of Dad's life was spent in a hospice room, with couches, a television and a mini-fridge. He had been in the room for four days, since he had gone into a coma-like state. Each of my five siblings and me, along with Mom, had taken time alone with Dad to say goodbye.

When it was my turn, language failed me. I wanted so badly to *tell him* — to have him understand everything that he meant to me. His genetics were imprinted on every cell within me. I have his height, his dark brown eyes, his taste for black pepper on field tomatoes. I have something of his essence too; his love for the poor and for travel, his restless spirituality. These — his body, his teachings, his way of being in the world — were my cornerstones. My life arose from his; my life would continue his.

But in those moments alone with him, I felt the full inadequacy of language. There was no word that held the sum of all that I felt; gratitude, grief, longing, despair, immense love. I did not yet know of the silent exchange that exists between two people who love each other. I did not know that this silent language was already at work.

In the end I said, "Dad, thank you for your love. I'm sorry for the times that I've hurt you. I hope you're proud of me. I'm proud to have you as my dad. Thank you for always loving me. I love you so much. Please stay with me. I'll always be with you."

As night fell, we felt sure it would be Dad's last. He had not had food or water for several days. Mom politely refused the request of my dad's two sisters who wanted to stay. My many aunts and uncles, all whom had travelled from the U.S., left after dinner. For some reason, Mom let me stay with her.

Night visited. In my memory, there is a rainstorm outside the window. We are shadows; Dad lying in light-coloured pyjamas, Mom on the couch praying and me, a girl with her head laid at the side of her dying father. I hovered there, between Mother and Father, light and dark, life and death, tangible and invisible; between this moment and the rest of my life.

Is this an accurate account of what transpired that night? I know within me, in the most important ways of knowing that a person can have, that the night was filled with a purity birthed only in the presence of great truths. And truth, in turn, seems to bathe itself in mystery.

But this, staying on an overnight vigil, is not what Peg means. Ellie begins to wait between breaths — five seconds, then seven, then nine — each one asking her to dig a little deeper inside of herself. Her lungs, her heart and body, are working hard. *The body knows how to die*, the hospice training manual read. It knows what systems to close first, where to stop expending energy. It's why the dying don't feel hungry and why mottled spots appear on bodies; digestion and circulation are no longer priorities. The body begins to withdraw all but the most essential functions. In its wisdom, the body hovers between its knowledge of dying and its programmed desire for life. At some point, the body surrenders and death prevails. It is a surrender to which we are each called.

Peg and I switch places. Peg moves to Ellie's left side and pulls up a chair. I stand at Ellie's right side, towards her up-tilted face. I bring mine close to hers and say, "Ellie, we're here. Peg and Anna are with you and we won't leave you. We won't leave." Then Peg, this shoot-from-the-hip, no-nonsense nurse who has witnessed so many deaths, begins to cry.

Something shifts and my whole self softens, every part of my body, my face, my insides. I sink into this moment. The deeper I settle, the more I am met with an arising clarity. Time slows and lengthens. My senses sharpen. I become acutely attuned to the invisible and magnificent power underpinning us. I breathe and Peg breathes and Ellie breathes. The whole room breathes and the earth does too, joining us in solidarity for this most important moment. One more human being is leaving the body; leaving the planet. I am both grounded and suspended at this tiny juncture of moving history. I feel soft and open and *so right here* with Ellie. I begin to smile. I can't seem to help it, so great is the comfort of this moment, its certainty and rightness, and my gratitude at the thousand circumstances that have allowed Peg and I to be present for it all.

Ellie's breaths become increasingly distant from one another and from us. I want to look at Peg, but I can't stop watching Ellie, her living and breathing through these moments of her dying. The contractions of her lungs. The contractions that are taking her away from us..

Finally, in the middle of this bed, in the centre of this room, adjacent to this nursing station on the western shores of Canada, planet Earth of the Milky Way galaxy, Eleanor Davis takes her last breath.

The three of us continue to hold hands. Peg's tears flow, washing us, providing a gentle river for Ellie's passing and carrying all of us to a new place. Reverence holds us. Then, Peg rises to the oxygen machine that is still pumping wet air.

"Peace," she says, turning it off. The room becomes so quiet. We are three women of different ages and stories, histories and lives who have come together for this short, momentous time.

Peg and I continue to breathe.

* * *

A few minutes pass. We begin to rouse as if coming out of yoga's *savasana*. *From the heavy hold of corpse pose, begin with gentleness to shift the body towards movement. Do not startle it awake, but provide it time to adjust; wiggle the toes, flex the feet, move the head gently from side to side. Let it be a slow enlivening as the sweetness of sleep slackens and drops from your limbs.*

Peg and I begin to move; a hand, a foot, a chair. Gradually, we are ushered out of *kairos* and returned to *chronos*. Peg stands and says that she needs to use the washroom and will let the nurse know that Ellie has died. This is my last moment alone with Ellie. I bend once more to her ear and whisper, *God love you, Ellie. Thank you.*

When Peg returns, the nurse is with her and asks, "How are you two doing? Was it peaceful?"

"Yes," we both agree. It was peaceful. We are okay. She tells us that she needs to do an assessment and some paperwork.

"Can I put the head down?" she asks, and Ellie is already gone. It's no longer *her head*, but *the head*. The bed is lowered and the nurse looks for vital signs. She documents Ellie's time of death: 4:35 p.m. She tells us that she will call the funeral home, but that they won't come for an hour. Woodhaven is required to keep a deceased person for at least that long. *Just in case*, she says.

We have some time. Peg calls Pastor Mark and leaves a message. I ask her what will happen now. Peg says that she will call Ellie's nephew in Manitoba when she gets home, but that it's not likely he'll come or want anything of Ellie's. She'll also contact Ellie's lawyer, who will hire someone to clean out Ellie and Ralph's trailer. All of their possessions will be donated or thrown away. The estate will be liquidated. Ellie's life, liquidated.

"Hi," Pastor Mark says, coming into the room. "I got here as quickly as I could." As always, he goes right to Ellie and picks up her hand. "Well Ellie, you're probably dancing right now." He asks us how her last minutes were. I ask if there will be a church service.

"I don't think so," Pastor Mark says. "She didn't want anything and there's no one here to have it for. Ralph was cremated and Ellie will be too, so maybe graveside prayers before the internment?"

I nod and ask them to please keep me informed, that I would like to attend if something is arranged. It seems unreal to me that there will be no service, no public acknowledgement of her life and death, and no one in this world outside of the three of us standing in this room who will miss her. It all seems to end here.

We begin to gather our things. Pastor Mark leaves for another appointment. Peg and I stand together one last time and look at Ellie. Peg turns to me and holds out her arms. We hug each other.

When we pull back, Peg says, "I am so grateful that you were here. It feels like this was the way it was supposed to be, with both of us with her. You really went above and beyond the role of a volunteer."

I tell her I feel the same. What was the likelihood that we were both here for Ellie's last hour? I tell her how much I appreciate her guidance and care for Ellie during the last few weeks. We both feel escorted by something hidden and holy. Peg and I exchange phone numbers and she promises to be in touch when she knows any service plans. We walk towards the door, stopping to thank the nurses for all of their care. I reach up and press the exit button. When the doors slide open, the sun is so bright that our eyes instinctively close.

The darkened space we leave behind has heightened the light's intensity. Soon our eyes will adjust, but for now we narrow our focus and allow just enough light in for this moment. Peg and I reach our cars and briefly hug again. As Peg climbs into the driver's seat, I notice the book she was reading sticking out from her purse. The title is *Hope*.

Climbing the stairs to the apartment, I am exhausted. When I reach the balcony I see that the potted Morning Glory has, on this day, flowered for the first time. A perfect blue bloom with a white star heart.

25

The Uses of Sorrow

(In my sleep I dreamed this poem)
Someone I loved once gave me
a box full of darkness.
It took me years to understand
that this too, was a gift.

The words were gifted to me by a holy man in the season of darkness. Advent: literally, *the coming, the arrival.* These are the days of dark that proceed Hanukkah and Christmas, celebrations of light.

The words crossed the quivering air and settled in my ears. At the precise moment of their settling, I understood immediately that a secret truth about my life had settled, too. I knew this only intuitively, the practical edges still to take shape. I had yet to understand that I would come to live these words only as they lived through me.

I had just completed my first chemotherapy regime and been declared cancer-free. It was a time weighted with patience, though hope lifted like curls of incense. As I sat in the darkened church lit with thin white candles, I hovered between illness and health, dark and light, waiting and arrival.

But in this first year, I was still *survivoring*, focused on escaping, dismantling and destroying cancer's box of darkness. *Weapons. Wage. War. Win. Warrior. Enemy. Armour. Army. Rally. Battle. Conquer. Destroy. Fight. Fight. Fight.* In those first months after diagnosis, the ideals of waging and winning a war did their job. Fear's adrenaline spawned intense action towards my survival. The language of war triggered me into doing more of what I was very good at — achieving positive outcomes. I applied this drive to surviving, directing my eating, exercise, emotional and spiritual life towards beating cancer. I prayed. I wrote a blog. People told me I was inspirational. To a degree, this language and the action it initiated protected me psychologically, providing something concrete in which to channel my panicked energy. In my situation of helplessness, this felt empowering and heroic. I did everything I could. I did everything right.

Then, I relapsed. Once. Twice. Three times. Each time was devastating in its own way, but the first time, I was also embarrassed. The cancer's return felt to be due to my lack of the emotional and spiritual strength to be free of disease. I, and others, wanted to believe that with the right mix of right actions, cancer would be overcome. Despite strategies and triumphant declarations, well-wielded weapons and mustered zeal, I had relapsed.

Powerlessness became unavoidable. It was the total defeat of my external doings, this revelation of powerlessness, that saved me.

One of the central differences between cancer cells and healthy cells is this: Cancer cells refuse to die. They grow rapidly, gobble resources, relentlessly divide. They invade areas to which they have no claim. They exploit the natural boundaries of life; the birth of being, the performance of duties, the necessity of dying. It is exactly these boundaries, the hedges of death, that help to give life its richness. Cancer shows contempt for life by attempting to circumvent its personal death.

What I came to slowly — painfully — realize was the extent to which these conditions controlled much of my life. The unwritten guidelines of frenzied doing, accumulation and achievement were embedded in me to the degree that not only could I not detect them, I defended and promoted them. Even after being diagnosed, even after having a 'socially acceptable' reason to rest, I had difficulty permitting myself to do so. I felt a good deal of anxiety and guilt over the fact that I felt reasonably well and even *enjoyed* my recovery time and caring for myself instead of keeping endlessly busy.

At times, I felt selfish, indulgent, and wasteful at my long hours of praying, resting and reading. When I was healthy, this anxiety didn't surface because ceaseless activity kept me feeling good, important, legitimatized. My energy was primarily concerned with the immediacy of *doing*, driven by a sense of *not-enoughness;* not working enough, not giving or earning enough. Certainly not *being* enough. Always operating from a sense of scarcity, I had to prove, to earn, to succeed, to expend myself at all cost. My illness, and the way I treated it, was no exception.

Cancer seemed to have mimicked this. My body had heard every thought I'd had over the duration of my lifetime, the thousands of silent evaluations of its parts and performances. It had endured my attempts to conform it to an imagined standard and suffered my pride when I thought it was achieved. I had sacrificed my Self on the altar of achievement, unknowingly perpetuating merciless activity in my soul. Cancer had not made my body a battleground. I had. And who was this enemy I was fighting? This enemy was me. I was being consumed by my own inability to stop.

This is a violent way of moving through the world both internally and externally. I felt little freedom to enjoy what I loved. I felt that *being good* meant denying what I naturally loved. Wasn't that true sacrifice? What I came to understand is that for me, this is where my ego hides — effectively concealed under the guise of *good*. My ego is self-serving when it sacrifices spirit in order to appear selfless. I was addicted to how others saw me.

This is my real woundedness, the place where I am vulnerable to forgetting that meaning is inherent in life and does not need to be manufactured. For others, this wound may be the need for perfection, uniqueness, achievement, control or constant connection.

All of this was taking place within my own flesh and within my own spirit. I had been living as a cancer cell, moving erratically through my own life, unconsciously silencing my unique life force and way of being in the world. I do not mean to say that in some way I caused my cancer, only that cancer became a microcosm of my life and a strong metaphor for aspects that I had neglected.

What cancer cannot see of itself is that its frantic rate of growth eventually kills the host on which it relies for its very life. Blind, unregulated, misdirected life force drives itself to death. As cancer attempted this on my body, ego attempted this on my soul. Cancer was not the box of darkness. Cancer was merely the scissors that opened the box.

These scissors had two blades: one stripped, one sharpened. Each blade was inscribed with a question that guided its work. The question of the first blade was: *When*

death comes, what of you will pass? And in the excruciating powerlessness of terminal illness, this blade performed like a
scythe. Painfully, the superficial and the excessive were sliced
from the substance of my life. Slowly, the fabricated sense of
who I was and what I was doing was shaved away.

What was the meaning of ceaseless work? Of cer-
tain relationships? Of the various activities that filled my day
and the endless goals that I pursued? Why did these often
appear meaningful but remain unsatisfying? And what of
the times I was too weak or sick to think about these? What
did these moments communicate about who I was and any
reason for being alive on this planet?

How bitter it was to see that upon the death of my
body, so many of the beliefs and activities I had so thoroughly thought of *as me* would also die. Though over time I came
to clearly know these as apparitions of the ego, I was pained
to let them go, having previously known them as allies and
intimates.

This letting go — this narrowing of what I thought
was me — was often terrifying. Along with the cancer and its
treatments, it left me feeling weak and withered. For a time,
several times, I felt as tender as a birdling, pink-raw and
chafed and afraid for the fall below. There was nothing I
could do until I could do nothing. For this blade fulfilled its
purpose: It hollowed me out. It made room. It brought me
to the purity of powerlessness. As the first blade finished its
work, the second arose to begin.

The edge of this blade was meant to sharpen. What
would fill this seeming void that had been created in me?
With my body, mind, emotions and spirit at their most vulnerable, what I desperately needed was tenderness, kindness,
compassion. I needed a strength that was not solely located

in the body. I needed a space within me unaffected by external change, a place that could not be intruded upon nor that needed legitimizing.

The guiding question of this blade was: *When death comes, what of you will last?*

Living with cancer — living, period — is more than simply avoiding death. Not even the best-trained doctors, most advanced tests or statistically-sound facts can fully predict the span or quality of my life. I will die. It may not be today or in 10 years or even from cancer, but someday, it will come. I committed myself to living a full life, if not a long one. In cosmic terms, *long* is not a remotely suitable description for the length of any human life, anyway.

I stopped thinking about my life in terms of *being cured* and instead began to wonder about *being healed*. Instead of waging war, I offered peace. I asked my body to forgive me for all of the ways I had broken its trust. I made choices for a simpler, more focused life, then made peace with the possibility of disappointing others. I stopped *should-ing* on myself. I did the things that felt good and right for me, and let go of the ones that didn't. I sank into being.

Because my healing involved emotional, mental and spiritual wellbeing, some of my choices involved a calculated risk, balancing my body's needs with the health of my soul. I missed events and some important trips, but I travelled too, especially to visit family. At other times, I needed to retreat from others, to turn inwards. This may have caused confusion or unintended hurt. I chose things that others may not. I can only say this: When it's your turn, I hope you'll get to choose what's right for you.

For me, real sacrifice looks more like accepting the messiness of life rather than continuously forcing it into an artificial perfection. Selflessness actually means caring for myself so that when I do act, it's from a place of genuine love and energy, instead of merely adding to the fretful exhaustion of the world. When in doubt, I tried to err on the side of love, to act in peace, to choose simplicity. These were subtle changes over time, ones that happened within me, in my thoughts and internal dialogue, in the way my movements slowed and my gestures softened. Perhaps it was not noticeable to others, but it changed the emphasis of my entire life.

Of great importance to me was to stop my attempts at weaponizing the holy. I had been given the well-intentioned advice that death was outside of God's plans for my life. Some believed that if I only wielded scripture and prayer in just the right ways, with just enough faith, that I would be cured. But death is not a defeat. It comes to the gods of every religion. Prayer, faith, love — these are inherently good and life-giving. Good things do not need to be manipulated, exploited, or forged into goodness. They simply are good. I believe in prayer and faith and love and God, not as a means to gain more years, but as life's own heart. Faith is not merely the means. It is the end itself.

In the moments of sickness and stillness, I began to feel a subtle shift, a certainty of knowing from within. It was not tied to particular events or happenings. It wasn't tied to reason. It was the growing impression, even in the midst of illness and death, *perhaps especially in the midst of illness and death*, that a type of guardianship encircled my life. This guardianship was both within me and beyond me. It did not rely on even my best spiritual insights or awakenings. It did not need my understanding nor my goodness. It exists for its own sake — love and love's fulfilment. There was nothing I needed to protect that wasn't already protected. I found my long-standing place of long-suffering trust, secure in the knowledge of both my eventual death and in the pervasive goodness that, nevertheless, underpins the whole of existence with its generous love.

Someone I loved...

Through all of this, in the dark descent to meet death, the ultimate paradox occurred. Life, the life within me and the life around me, revealed itself with a vibrancy and multiplicity I had not yet experienced. It came with a distilled sense of clarity. Life became more joyful and deeply peaceful. There was greater tenderness and more elation. I was alive in ways I could not have been without death beside me. These moments of acuity became more frequent, more habituated within me. I could access them when alone, in a crowd, or even lying on a scanning machine. From this field laid waste by suffering, my spirit arose and ran free in delight. I have never felt closer to God, to others, to love.

Someone I loved gave me a box full of darkness...

Sometimes I miss the simple clarity of that time as a mystic misses the all-too-brief euphoria of divine unity or as I sometimes miss those early days with Andrew, when all was blissful novelty. But as the mystic and the devoted spouse and the lifelong friend knows, those brief feelings eventually subside and stabilize into a love that is more steadfast, profound and enduring.

It took me years to understand...

It takes courage to forgive reality for not being perfect, seemingly just or even remotely fair. It takes courage to accept life on its own terms. It takes courage to be conscious. It takes courage now, to remember cancer even when it has retreated enough to allow me reprieve. It takes courage to remember its lessons and to remain awake.

I do not know why there is such joy and such suffering and how they can be simultaneously held by this world. I can only open my heart and let it be broken over and over in order to be cleared out, transformed, and brought to more love.

And this fulcrum — where *what will pass* meets *what will last*, when stripped then sharpened, when body and being are broken open in heartache and brought back together in greater love — this fulcrum is no less than a pivot of grace.

This is survivorship — surviving the death of all that is not me and living in the love that will last; trusting that in my last bodily moments, it will be enough. Suffering is not, in itself, redemptive. It is the *transformation of suffering* into love, joy and beauty, in service to the divine and to life, that is salvation. It is Love's purpose, and mine. It is ours.

...*this too, was a gift.*

26

Terminal:
Of, or relating to, an end, extremity or boundary;
The end of the line;
Ultimately leading to death.

Year 6

Have you ever sat with your hand on your belly? Have you ever closed your eyes and felt the air of this universe come into your nose, tingle through your lungs and gently push your tummy out against the warmth of your palm? Have you ever watched your body softly rise and fall, realizing — truly understanding — that you are alive at this exact moment in history?

It's enough to make you cry.

* * *

As promised, the nurse called the morning after my father's birthday. After I hung up the phone with her, I put my mouth to the couch and screamed. Over and over, a wail that Andrew later told me he had never before heard from a human being. Our superintendent crept to the apartment door, drawn by the sound of someone in his building, dying.

* * *

I walked to the gym and told the girl behind the desk: *I'd like to cancel my membership.*

Can I ask why?

I'm not using it and I'm back and forth to Toronto a lot.

Oh, well you can upgrade your membership and use it anywhere in Ontario.

Thank you, but no, I think I'll cancel.

But you've been a member for three years and have a great rate!

How to say this politely? Listen, I have a life-threatening illness and might be dying. The last of my days don't include listening to your sales pitch. Please just cancel the damned membership.

I went home and dropped my courses for the term, not even opening the books I ordered online and had just arrived in the mail. Instead, I used my pen to update my Power of Attorney and Personal Care Directive.

All lost pieces of the living Anna.

* * *

On my walks, I watched the wind bend the tree branches. Seeds fell onto the ground where the birds came to eat. I said to the wind and the tree, to the birds and the seed and the whole earth under me: *I am coming.*

* * *

The phone call told me that the tissue removed from my lung was, in fact, cancer. I was discharged from the bone marrow transplant clinic as *we have pulled out our big guns and there is nothing more to offer from our end.* I was referred to Princess Margaret Hospital's lymphoma specialist. I had a scan that showed the cancer was both above and below my diaphragm in multiple spots. *I can get you into remission,* the lymphoma doctor said. *I'm just not sure how long you'll stay there.*

My years of internal work seemed for nothing. I felt a great deal of anguish all of the time. Andrew woke throughout the night to make sure I was breathing. I said to him, *I just want something durable, something permanent. What would you do if you had a year to live? How would you make it meaningful? What can I invest in so deeply that it will continue to exist after I die?*

He reminded me, again. *You don't have to do anything to make this year meaningful. There's nothing that could make it more meaningful than it is already. Living your life, preparing for death, talking about it, loving and caring for others. There is nothing more meaningful than all of that.*

* * *

Andrew wrote this in his journal: *Would you change anything about your life if you were told you might die in a year? It is a hypothetical question for most. Anna was told by her oncologist that it's likely that she does not have long to live. Here is a list, in no particular order, of some of the things she decided to do:*

Visit her family. Eat chocolate. Live by the ocean. Give away most of her possessions. Read. Write. Send mail to her nieces and nephews. Go to funerals. Volunteer. Walk. Cook. Meditate. Get married. Pray. Give thanks. Encourage. Cry. Love, and so on.

* * *

There was a possibility of a new therapy, a targeted drug engineered to locate and attack only cancer cells, leaving hair and gut cells alone and the immune system largely intact. The drug had promising initial results for keeping lymphoma in remission, though for how long, no one was certain. The problem was that though it was approved for use in Ontario, its cost was not yet covered by the healthcare system. At an estimated $10,000 a dose, the doctor suggested we wait a few weeks to see if it became funded.

A month later, the drug came under the provincial healthcare coverage and I began taking brentuximab vedotin. I also approached the bone marrow clinic doctors in Toronto to request a Donor Lymphocyte Infusion (DLI). A DLI is a 'top-up' of donor cells that has the potential to reactivate the graft vs. lymphoma effect. The doctors were hesitant as it also has the potential to trigger severe GvHD. They finally agreed, and in the coming months, I had two DLI's without any GvHD.

Brentuximab vedotin was developed as a treatment for relapsed lymphoma with a one-year dosage recommendation. After one-year, scans showed I had no detectable signs of cancer and my doctor agreed to extend the treatment. I remained on brentuximab vedotin for two years until I began having neuropathy in my feet from its longterm use.

27

Cradle:
A newborn's bed, designed to soothe;
A rocking device used in panning for gold;
A framework for healing;
A place of origin.

Year 7
Me, Ellie and Dad; All of Us

A week goes by and I don't hear from Peg or Pastor Mark. The local paper gets printed but doesn't hold any mention of Ellie's passing. On the eighth day after Ellie dies, I pull out Peg's phone number and dial. After three rings, I prepare to leave a message when she answers.

"Hi Peg," I say. "It's Anna. How are you doing? I'm just wondering if you've heard anything more about Ellie."

"Oh, hi Anna. I'm sorry I haven't called you. I don't know much yet. I've been on the phone with her nephew. He decided against an announcement in the paper. Thought it would let people know her place was empty. He's not going to bother coming so I turned the keys over to the lawyer. The lawyer said he will hire someone to sort the trailer contents and either donate or get rid of them. I told him I don't want anything to do with that.

"In terms of Ellie, I know the funeral home picked her up and she was cremated. Pastor Mark is away for the next week, so I won't know anything until he gets back. I know he mentioned a small graveside service, but I'm not sure who would attend. I think the funeral home will keep her for up to three weeks." Peg lets out a long sigh. "So that's it, I guess. I'm sorry I haven't called, but there wasn't much news to tell."

"That's okay," I say. "I just wondered if anything had happened or been decided. I wondered how it all wrapped up. I'd definitely be interested in attending, if there is a service."

"Well, I'll talk to Pastor Mark as soon as he gets back and give you a call either way." I tell her that would be great, that I'd really appreciate it.

"And Peg?" I say before the call ends, "Thanks again for everything. It was a pleasure to be with you. You and Ellie."

"For me too, Anna. For me, too."

I hang up and look down at the silent phone. The remainder of Ellie's presence on this earth is out of my hands.

I don't hear from Peg again.

* * *

Another week goes by, bringing with it a sense of restlessness. Andrew is going to work for a few hours, so I ask him to drop me near Martyr Mountain. I will hike to the top and do a short meditation before returning to the base where he will pick me up after his shift.

The community's cemetery lies at the base of the mountain, so I decide to first walk the grounds to look for Ellie's husband's headstone. Then I will know where she will be interned.

The cemetery is modest, hedged on two sides by forest and on the other two by quiet, out-of-the-way roads. The grass is thick and trim. Aged trees twist up from the ground, marking progressively newer sections of headstones. The graves are well-tended and set with bursts of flowers. A few wood-slated benches await an occupant.

Cemeteries are history books, stories of those who have inhabited a tiny span of earth and time. Each headstone is a chapter title, an abridgement of the character below. Together, these chapters tell the narrative of a place and a people. This particular cemetery is the story of immigrants to the area. The original peoples of this land maintain their own burial grounds.

The context is set by the oldest headstones closest to the road. Many belong to Italian immigrants who came to the area in the late 19th- and early 20th-centuries to work in the pulp and paper mill. These graves are marked with tall crosses, ornate designs cut into the cold stone. *Nato. Morto. In Memoria.* Many are being claimed by soft, moist moss.

I move slowly, pay attention, do justice to this place. Towards the edge of the first section, the epitaphs begin to read such things as *The One We Loved; Budded on Earth to Bloom in Heaven; Blest be the ties that bind.* It is an area for children. On many, the word *Baby* is given in place of a name, the day of *Baby's* birth and death the same. Others lived one, three or five years. There is a headstone that shares the names of triplet girls. *Your lost lives are grieved.* I read every inscription.

Bodies of babies in the ground seems irreconcilable. I imagine the silhouettes of the many guardians who have stood where I stand, staring at the soil, the damp and grassy plot that is their child's body. The burial ground of hope but not of love — never of love — forever soaked by their endless grief. I think of a nephew, a 4-year-old boy of whom I think of all days, and whose story awaits another writer.

I continue. The cemetery is small, but scanning the stones, it takes me the better part of an hour to reach the newest section. I wonder if I've somehow missed Ralph's name. Then, in the last row, I find it. I find them. Ellie's name has already been set on the shared headstone, her date of death yet unentered. Underneath their names is a one-line inscription: *Always in our hearts.* I stare down at it until my eyes water. Between Ellie and Ralph and the mountain is an open field designated for future tenants. The longer I live here, the more people I will know, and the more this particular piece of earth will become part of my own story.

On the outer rim of the cemetery, at the base of the mountain, conifers rise to the sky; shoulder-to-shoulder sentinels, an honour guard for the dead. From their steeples, the wind, a hawk, a God, keeps mindful eye.

There are blackberry bushes here, heavy with ripe fruit. A handful, crushed in the cavity of my living mouth; picked and crushed until my hands and mouth become stained with deep purple substance. I marvel at the size of them, recognizing that the land that brings them to this bursting ripeness is the land of reclaimed remains.

Infused with this salvaged energy, I find the trail and begin to climb. It is a steep ascent. I am a tiny smudge among trunks thickened by time. I climb towards their crowns.

I think of my experience with Ellie, knowing it was eased by many factors. Hers was not a young death, nor a painful one, nor one due to cancer. She had no family but wanted visitors, which allowed a measure of comfort and liberty as to how we spent our time together. And too, Ellie was at peace with death. The circumstances of Ellie's death were neither heroic nor horrific, except in the ways in which all deaths are. We want one and fear the other, but in reality, most deaths hold these in tension.

More than once I've wondered if it is irreverent, a trespass, to record these last happenings of Ellie's life. It is a privileged position to witness, even from a ways off, someone travelling the road of their dying. I do not want to exploit my time with Ellie, nor my position with her. I saw only the tip of Ellie's iceberg. The bulk of her life   her childhood and family life, her preferences, desires, and thoughts, and even her eating and walking — was already below the surface of the years.

Yet I was privy to, and privileged by, the sweet depths of her finality. I heard her final sentences and saw her last gestures. I watched how her body embraced its conclusion, saw something of its shakes and swelling, paling skin and pooling blood, its increased difficulty in simply staying alive. I watched for dry skin and bed sores and grew to know the mouth that opened and closed without purpose. The way she pushed away the hair on her forehead or waved her hand when she couldn't find the word she wanted to say, became familiar. I was fond of the soft, crushed look of her earlobe. Though at times I am still unsure if this writing will be seen as a tribute or an intrusion, it feels a gift I can give to Ellie, *the forever Ellie* that I came to know.

I clear the base and meet the rough rock staircase fashioned along the jaw of the mountain. The trees are so thick here that the ground is perpetually damp. I take the rail. My breath becomes my labour. I walk. I walk and walk and *w-awe-k*, beginning to metabolize the grief from my cells, all of the things I have seen and heard and absorbed within me.

Bowels. Bells. Urine output. Oxygen intake. Sobs. Held breaths. Cooling fingers. Fevers. Blood-drained faces, blood-pooled bruises. Injections. Questions. Decisions. Supply carts. Never enough. Sanitizer, plastic dishes, florescent lights. Stories of childhood, of mischief and dinner tables. Salmon piled in the mouths of bears and on hungry tree roots. Hair, shaved from scalps. Ellie's head, lowered down. They have come through my senses — my mouth, nose, ears, eyes and touch — and have settled in me as pockets of grief.

Walking begins to stir these, loosening them from my bones and flesh. Clearing, digesting, freeing, releasing and mixing pine, salt, prisms, wind, dirt, water, wine. I pull in the exhales of the trees, the breath of this living body that vitalizes the earth. My lungs pull this breath into every nook of me, steeping my cells in life. Somehow inside the mystery of my body, this breath is alchemized into a breath for plants. I exhale it in thanks.

This is creation's dynamic and intimate alliance, a covenant signed at my conception. It fostered my rise from the ground of my ancestors and has fed me since birth. Someday, it will ask me to make good on my end of the bargain. When that day comes, I will descend to the earth that produced my body and readies for it again. This marrow of me, created from air and lichen and blackberries and one day, given back for them. I take the raw materials of life into myself not only for survival but to transform them for the benefit of all.

Ellie's first words, *I've had diarrhea all night*, brought me to the feet of our shared humanity. All of the characters we play in life, the positions we are known for and function in, the achievements for which we are rewarded — will cease to be in the moment of our death. What will last, what will forever reside and resound, is what is done in love. Somehow, through my illness and hers, pain became growth, descent became arising, and death became redemption. If you are at all ordained in your lifetime with great suffering or great love, you will begin to understand and to live these truths while you still breathe, not awaiting the moment of death to awaken you to your own life.

For Ellie and me, this mutual understanding blessed the space between us. We lived and breathed together on this planet and found our way to an imperishable fellowship. I learned that we not only transform oxygen and energy but that we are responsible to participate in the transfiguration of all we are given — *including and especially suffering* — for the sake of love.

Near the top of the mountain, I clear the tree line. Here, I belong to the sky. I see the Pacific and her islands, shorebirds on beaches, rocks formed into both cliff and cornerstone, and earth's beard of trees. I find a mossy spot and sit, looking over the patch of land that Mom and Dad had hoped to see. Here I am — living out their dreams. I take out the small jar I have stored in my pocket. I often wonder how Dad would have handled my cancer diagnosis. It may have killed him more quickly than his own. I gently loosen the lid and tip the jar to the breeze. The breath of the earth catches the ashes and joyfully whirls them east, towards home.

> I don't know exactly what a prayer is.
> I do know how to pay attention,
> how to fall down into the grass,
> how to kneel down in the grass,
> how to be idle and blessed...
>
> Tell me, what else should I have done?
> Doesn't everything die at last, and too soon?
>
> Tell me,
> what is it you plan to do
> with your one wild and precious life?[3]

And so, seven years after initial diagnosis, here I am, stained hands and sweetened mouth. I let the ocean overtake me and behold! — I did not drown. Instead, I washed up on a distant shore, cleansed and falling down, blessed. I don't know exactly what a prayer is, but I want to live as though my life *is* the prayer. I want to live in the *Love, and so on.* This is the only way I know to honour my one wild and precious life. *You do what you can. Let God do the rest.*

The sky breaks open before me, a cathedral at the cross-planks of life and death, joy and pain, loss and love, divinity and humanity.

Always remember, he said. *Take care of one another.*

---

[3] Mary Oliver.

BIBLIOGRAPHY

Lynn, Robert L. "Cancer Is So Limited." *Cancer Is So Limited and Other Poems of Faith.* CreateSpace Independent Publishing Platform, 2013.

Oliver, Mary. "The Summer Day." *House of Light.* Boston, MA: Beacon Press, 1990.

Oliver, Mary. "The Uses of Sorrow." *Thirst.* Boston, MA: Beacon Press, 2005.

Tillich, Paul. *Systematic Theology, Volume I.* Chicago, IL: University of Chicago Press, 1973.

ABOUT THE AUTHOR

The unifying principle of Anna's personal and professional experiences is a deep regard for, and devotion to, the inherent dignity of individuals, especially those who are most vulnerable. A theological student and past educator, she has worked as a teacher of adolescents with mental health challenges and adults with physical and cognitive disabilities. Raised in a Roman Catholic Irish family, Anna explored Protestantism in her 20s and later, the perennial wisdom shared by many spiritual traditions. She has studied with Fr. Richard Rohr, Cynthia Bourgeault and James Finley at the Center for Action and Contemplation in Albuquerque, New Mexico. She has a combined degree in psychology and gerontology from McMaster University. She is the coordinator for a hospice society in coastal British Columbia.